ORGANIC VEGETABLE GARDENING

How to Grow Your Vegetables and Start a Healthy Garden at Home.
A Step-by-Step Guide for Beginners (2022)

Howell Mcbride

TABLE OF CONTENT

Introduction

Never before has the time been more opportune to take on the joyful challenge of growing your own vegetables at home—organically and healthfully. This book will walk you through the entire process, from the fundamentals of why and how to the rewarding activities of harvesting and preserving.

First, we'll go over what it means to garden organically, why it's important, and how to do it simply and skillfully. Then we'll get down to business, preparing the soil and sourcing the seeds to get the garden off to a good start. Next, decide what vegetables and herbs to grow is obviously fundamental and, without a doubt, a big part of the fun of gardening; one of the pleasures of having one is customizing it. Once the foundation is in place, preparing for the inevitable—if you build it, the pests will come—becomes a necessary task, albeit one that is more welcome than it may appear at first. As you begin to garden, you will discover that dealing with garden pests brings out the best in many of us.

Following that, we'll look at the best ways to keep your garden healthy throughout the growing season, as well as how to harvest and use your harvest. This includes some suggestions for simple recipes as well as longer-term storage: Finding a bag of vine-ripened roasted tomatoes in your freezer in the middle of February is like capturing the summer sun. Of course, maintaining a garden through all four seasons is ideal.

Finally, a look back at what has been accomplished and the impact it has on our lives and the world: Growing your own vegetable garden is a wonderful way to sustain yourself and all those you love, from the backyard to the table.

Chapter One

THE FUNDAMENTALS OF WHY AND HOW: ORGANIC 101

What Exactly Is Organic Gardening?

Under the auspices of the National Organic Program (NOP), the United States Department of Agriculture determines the definition and regulation of how the term "organic" is used and labeled in our food supply. Simply put, organic foods are those that have been grown or raised without the use of genetically modified organisms (GMOs), sewer sludge (many industrial farms water their crops with treated sewage runoff), or irradiation (in the case of meat products).

The NOP also requires organic crops to be grown without the use of petroleum-based or other synthetic fertilizers and pesticides, though these rules are subject to change every five years, and the NOP has been chastised for allowing small amounts of synthetic materials to be used under the label "organic." The NOP also manages the nationwide certification program that allows farms to earn the "certified organic" label. However, because the certification process is time-consuming and expensive, many smaller farms, such as those that sell at local farmers' markets, may follow the regulations for growing organic crops but do not hold a certification. Simply ask your farmer what kind of chemicals and methods he or she uses at their farm if you buy at local farmers' markets, which I encourage you to do because most home gardeners cannot grow everything they might want for their table.

Even if a local farmer sprays a common pesticide once a year, it is far healthier than purchasing an industrially farmed product that is constantly sprayed. For the home gardener, it all boils down to this: to garden organically, simply avoid synthetic fertilizers in favor of natural ones, such as compost (discussed in the following chapter), and synthetic pesticides.

One would assume that the home gardener does not need to be concerned about sewer sludge, though locating your gardening away from community ponds or parks is always a good idea because areas maintained by communities or government-run entities frequently use synthetic materials; avoiding runoff ensures that your garden maximizes its healthy, organic potential.

Why Plant Organically?

The ills of industrial agriculture are well documented, as most of us are well aware. Petroleum-based fertilizers and pesticides are harmful to the environment—the soil, the air, and groundwater—as well as a non-renewable resource fraught with political implications based on how and where oil is obtained. Furthermore, most of us are aware that the health costs of eating chemically laden produce are unquestionably high, particularly for children. "I would not feed my children a non-organic apple," said a pediatrician I once knew.

Other factors involved in the industrial production of our food supply are worth mentioning and should cause us to reconsider our food choices. Examples include the simple matter of taste, the imprint of our carbon footprint, the dangers of monocultures, the unknown threats posed by GMOs, and the unseen costs of human rights violations.

Taste

While many may argue that taste is subjective and a matter of personal preference, I defy anyone to compare a homegrown, vine-ripened tomato to a supermarket tomato and give the backyard version a negative review. Supermarket tomatoes have been bred for hardiness, so they can be easily harvested and shipped long distances, rather than taste. They are typically picked while green to allow for the use of machine harvesters, which essentially knock unripe tomatoes to the ground while ripe tomatoes splat, and shipped in trucks that spray them with manufactured ethylene gas to make them appear "ripe."

You are purchasing an unripe, sour, bland tomato that has been mechanically coaxed into blushing slightly. While the tomato is used as an example here, the concept can easily be applied to any number of vegetables and fruits that are grown for convenience rather than flavor.

Carbon Footprint

As the preceding example shows, shipping becomes a primary concern in industrial agriculture. Unless you live in parts of California or Florida, the majority of our produce is grown elsewhere. Thus, our fruits and vegetables are grown for hardiness not only against disease or pests but also against the rigors of shipping. So, the average American table's carbon footprint is quite concerning: fertilizers and pesticides notwithstanding, the amount of oil used in transportation is staggering. In fact, industrial agriculture is the second largest contributor to greenhouse gas emissions, trailing only the energy industry.

Monocultures

Another risk associated with intensive farming, which is a hallmark of industrial agriculture, is the formation of monocultures. This is when a specific crop, usually a single strain, is grown extensively across a large area of land. The traditional American farm consisted of a variety of crops as well as livestock that worked in tandem: the fertilizer produced by the livestock nurtured the variety of produce grown, which in turn fed both the animals and the family.

On modern industrial farms, one product is grown exclusively — think of Kansas' wheat fields (now mostly soybean fields), which stretch as far as the eye can see. This is true not only for grain crops, but also for tomatoes, apples, citrus, and a variety of other fruits and vegetables.

Monocultures pose a risk because when one crop is grown intensively in one area, it depletes the soil of nutrients and makes it more susceptible to disease. For example, in recent years, disease has virtually wiped out banana crops grown intensively in tropical regions: when one strain of banana, the Cavendish, supplanted most other strains, the crops became vulnerable to a fast-spreading fungal invasion. Monocultures are always in jeopardy of extinction.

Genetically Modified Organisms
While the effects of widespread use of genetically modified organisms (GMOs) are still largely unknown, the dangers present in monoculture farming are similar to those created by GMO farming, including disease susceptibility and soil depletion. Furthermore, the use of GMOs brings with it a slew of other potential threats, not the least of which is the invasiveness of some of these crops.For example, Monsanto developed a genetically modified corn crop that was so successful that its seeds spread to other fields across the country, choking out more traditional breeds.

It should be noted that this particular strain of corn was bred to resist the weed killer Roundup (referred to as "Roundup ready," several crops have been genetically modified in this manner); this allowed farmers to spray their fields with weed killer throughout the growing season without harming the corn (or canola, or soybean, etc.). Furthermore, Monsanto patents these products, which means that farmers cannot use them without paying for them—and must buy new seeds every year, as the plant is also bred to be sterile—and at least one farmer has been sued by the corporation because Roundup ready plants were discovered in his field, contaminating his seeds with the GMO version.

Thus, the increasing use of GMOs represents a continuing intensification of corporate control over our farms and crops, as well as potential health risks. The FDA does not require human testing before approving GMO crops, and products containing GMOs are not required to be labeled.

Labor Issues

The last problematic symptom of industrial agriculture's ills is one of the least discussed and largely unseen concerns: human rights violations. While many of us are aware that migrants perform a large portion of agricultural labor that has not been mechanized, few are aware of the conditions that many of these laborers must endure. Many of the migrant workers in the field are women.

They could be considered indentured servants. These vulnerable men and women are lured onto farms with promises of decent pay for hard work, but they end up paying exorbitant rents for shacks with no running water or electricity while earning only a few dollars per day. Bosses frequently give them "advances" on their meager pay so that the laborers can buy food or liquor, leaving them in debt. There have also been reports of workers being physically abused if they do not move quickly enough or work hard enough. Tomatoland, Barry Estabrook's comprehensive account of the tomato-farming industry, exposes in detail what goes on at some farms.

Having said that, the benefits of organic home gardening appear clear: you can avoid the potential health risks of petrochemical exposure as well as the ethical quandaries involved in industrial agriculture practices while growing much tastier, more beautiful, and more satisfying food. The benefits to yourself, your family, and the environment cannot be overstated, and even the smallest garden can have a significant impact. So, let us deal with the logistics and get started right away!

How Do You Grow Organically?

Even if you've never gardened before, doing so organically isn't too difficult, though knowing a few ground rules helps. And, if you've previously gardened but want to do so more healthfully now, the transition will be especially simple. In the following chapter, we will delve deeper into the fundamentals of organic gardening, but first, let us consider what we might need to consider in order to get a garden of any kind growing.

First and foremost, any serious gardener should invest in high-quality tools. For advice and products, go to your local gardening emporium or, if necessary, a big box mart for convenience and cost-effectiveness. A handy list of some basic tools you should get is provided below.

Small Shed

While this may not be necessary for the lucky gardener who has plenty of convenient, unutilized garage space, it will become essential for many of us. If you garden in your backyard, as many of us do, and have a garage in the front, a storage shed on the back porch can be a huge time saver.

Not only will everything be easily accessible, but this arrangement also facilitates organization. Plastic sheds are relatively inexpensive and can be purchased at any number of garden centers. I went without for my first two gardening seasons and was amazed at how much more efficient (and less irritated) I became by getting one and keeping it well organized.

Gloves

These are at the top of my list because their significance cannot be overstated. Gardening with a missing fingernail or cuts all over your hands is difficult (though getting some dirt under the nails can make one feel accomplished). I'd recommend several types of gloves: a thin pair of washable gloves for fine weeding and planting seeds; latex gloves for wet jobs or weeding among thorny plants; and a pair of heavy leather gloves for tough jobs like digging large holes, moving soil, or raking. If you have sensitive skin (cucumber and tomato vines are prickly), you may want to invest in some elasticized arm protectors (or an old long-sleeved shirt and some sturdy rubber bands).

Shovels

Round-headed shovels are ideal for general-purpose work such as digging holes and moving soil or compost. To extend its life, choose a sturdy one and keep it clean after use. Steelheads are typically more durable than aluminum heads.

Rakes

There are two kinds of long-handled rakes that are useful for a lightweight leaf rake for raking leaves and grass clippings, and a bow rake for leveling soil and spreading compost and mulch in general. A hand rake is also useful for close work in the vegetable garden, such as removing debris from around the base of a plant without damaging the stalks or roots.

Hand trowel

For digging small, precise holes for planting and close weeding. A Japanese hori-hori knife can be used in the same way as a hand trowel, with the added benefit of having a saw blade for dividing young plants.

Shears and Scissors

A good pair of shears is especially useful at the end of the gardening season to cut down any dead or dying vines; it is also great for pruning if you have larger items in your garden to tackle, such as hedges. A sturdy pair of scissors is essential for clipping tender herbs and pruning back delicate plants in the garden.

Pruners

While a good pair of shears and scissors will suffice for most vegetable gardening, a strong pruner will be required when growing larger plants and bushes. It can be used to cut thicker branches and to prune trees if you get one with a long handle.

Transplant Spade

This tool is similar to a larger, longer-handled trowel and is useful when transplanting a large number of young plants at once. If you intend to have a large garden, this is a must. A digging fork is used to move and turn over loose soil. There are forks with short and long handles. I prefer a short-handled one for close work and a bow rake for most other tasks.

Watering Solutions

The garden hose is the most basic watering tool for the casual backyard gardener, and it will work for any gardener who has the time to water thoroughly. For a few years, it worked well with a handheld watering can and a water breaker attachment (which provides a gentle even flow of water to avoid damaging plants). But, when I finally purchased a soaker system, also known as drip irrigation, I was pleased and relieved: simply turning on the hose for 30 minutes in the morning (and another 30 in the early evening during hot weather) did the trick while I could do other things. This is a more expensive option, but for the serious home gardener, especially if you live in a drought-prone area, it is well worth it.

Composting Solutions

If you truly want to garden organically, you must purchase some kind of composter. There are numerous models on the market, with prices ranging from low to high, and from small indoor to large outdoor. While most of these models are simple and efficient, you can also make your own composter with a few simple items. The fundamentals of composting are covered in detail in the following chapter. Second, it is beneficial for the home gardener to have some reliable resources on hand for advice and troubleshooting, such as this book! Aside from this book, there are a few other resources available to most home gardeners.

Local Stores

While online shopping cannot be matched in terms of ease and convenience, it is still important to remember that your local store can provide specific and useful advice. Typically, the proprietor is familiar with the area and what works best in that area. As well, frequenting a particular business with regularity forms a lasting relationship, wherein a past purchase leads to a present conversation which prevents a future problem.

Farmers' Markets

If you have the pleasure of enjoying a farmers' market in your area, it is in your best interest to frequent it and become acquainted with your local farmers. Most farmers at the market are big supporters of backyard gardens, seeing them as partners in a project to make the world a healthier and more environmentally friendly place. They also have a lot of knowledge and will often gladly share it with you. Furthermore, many farmers welcome visitors to their farms, and if your market has any organic farm stands, I encourage you to visit and ask lots of questions.

They can help you with almost any aspect of farming, from knowing what and when to plant to knowing how much and when to water, fighting disease and pests, and harvesting and preparing what you grow. And you can get many lovely vegetables and fruits (as well as humanely produced meat, eggs, milk, cheese, and honey) that you don't have in your backyard.

Co-op Research and Extension Services

Through their co-op and extension services, the USDA sponsors a nationwide network of agricultural resources. Essentially, it assists local cooperatives—farms, educational institutions, markets, and other cooperative businesses—in agricultural and human health research and development. If you live near a Land-Grant institution, you are probably close to an extension service, which houses local cooperative members to help with disseminating knowledge throughout the community on topics such as sustainable agriculture and food safety and quality. These resources can assist you by testing the pH of your soil. For example, offering organic gardening seminars or bringing together local gardeners to form a support network. If you don't live near an extension service, there are resources available online. Links can be found at https://www.usda.gov/topics/rural/cooperative research-and-extension-services.

Third, you must challenge yourself to put words into action: now that you have the tools and resources to get started, the next two chapters will walk you through the process of establishing your garden, from preparing the soil and handling seeds to deciding which plants go well together. Let us answer the call of the great outdoors!

Chapter Two

GETTING STARTED WITH SOIL AND SEEDS

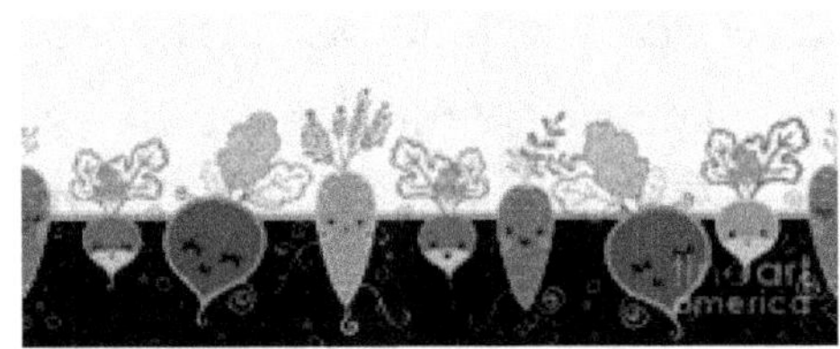

The first step in starting a garden is to find a suitable location with a solid foundation; depending on where you live, there are several options. Then, concentrate on the soil; optimizing compost and other organic fertilizers to create a rich and bountiful bed for your vegetables is one of the keys to successful organic gardening. Once you've chosen your location and prepared your soil, you can begin collecting seeds, nurturing seedlings, and dealing with transplants.

Building A Solid Foundation

Where you live often dictates how you set up your garden. For many of us, the backyard is the best place to start a garden, but you can also successfully garden on a balcony or terrace, or even indoors. One of your first considerations should be light exposure, as most vegetable plants require some direct sunlight during the growing season. Indoor gardening, can be accomplished by using a sunny windowsill or, less appealing but effective, grow lights.

If you want to start a garden in your backyard, you must first determine the size of your plot. I began with a small 8' by 4' plot for herbs, chiles, and a few tomato plants, then expanded to a 12' by 4' plot for lettuces, peas, beans, and a variety of other vegetable plants. The size is entirely up to you, depending on your yard and how much you want to grow in the garden.

Also, while you can certainly follow some tips for maximizing space (addressed throughout this book), you must also be mindful not to overcrowd. For example, direct seed young lettuces in your garden while tending to tomato and chile seedlings indoors; once your lettuces are harvested — they will not withstand the heat of summer — transplant your seedlings. Other plants, such as garlic, are good for overwintering after the garden has reached its peak of production in the summer.

Understanding your area's climate or USDA Plant Hardiness Zone is another factor to consider when planning your garden. The United States is divided into 11 zones, which essentially track average temperatures across the country, with Zone 1 having the coldest average temperatures and Zone 11 having the warmest (click here for a link to the most current USDA map). However, the zone map does not necessarily track weather patterns other than temperature, nor does it take into account the effects of altitude on the growing season. Still, it gives you a good idea of which plants are most common suitable for your area, as well as when various crops might be planted. This is where a resource like a local garden shop or extension service (discussed in the previous chapter) can help. I've mostly gardened in Zone 7 and have long followed the local wisdom of not planting delicate seedlings before tax day; there's always the possibility of an unexpected freeze around Easter.

Another thing to consider is the quality and type of soil in your area (obviously, we'll go over how to improve this later, but it's important to know where you're starting from), as well as rainfall averages. This will determine whether you can simply till up a plot of land in your backyard, add some compost and organic fertilizer, and garden as is. Raised bed gardens, on the other hand, make more sense in many, if not most, cases.

The raised bed garden has the advantage of allowing water to drain more effectively through the soil—especially if you live in clay-based soil—and delineates a specific area for your garden, rather than the entire backyard. It also means that you have more effective control over the quality of soil in which you grow your vegetables; this may be a concern in heavily suburban areas where contamination of the soil by lawn care and other factors—public parks, ponds, golf courses—is a concern. A raised bed also allows for more even sunlight distribution.

There are numerous raised bed options available for purchase, some of which are raised so high that the need to bend over is eliminated (though these are for very small-scale operations, for the most part). You can also make your own with a little creativity and extra effort. I like to get untreated, rot-resistant wood planks from a good local source and shingle them together until the bed is about 12" from the subsoil once filled with compost and soil.

A good drill and some rebar can be used to secure this bed to the ground, with the added benefit of allowing you to put up some kind of fencing to keep small animals out. Keep the raised bed narrow so that you don't have to walk into the garden, and if you put up fencing, include a small gate for easy access to the interior when needed.

Two other issues to consider when establishing a garden, raised bed or not, are how to get rid of grass, should you be planting in a yarded area, and how to effectively water. It is certainly possible to remove grass by cutting out sod and rolling it away, but it is not very practical for the home gardener. What is easier, though not foolproof, is to line your garden bed with cardboard or landscaping fabric before adding your topsoil — but if your concerns are to remain truly organic, make sure to check what these products are made of or treated with.

Mulch is another effective grass deterrent; keeping a nice layer of organic mulch throughout the garden after planting not only prevents excessive grass growth but also helps to retain moisture and maintain temperature.

Consider how you intend to water your garden when planning it. Installing a drip irrigation system at the start of the growing season is highly recommended, but not required. Drip irrigation, soaker hoses, and spot watering emitters save water more effectively than spraying a garden with your hose and save a lot of time throughout the growing season.

Another factor to consider when designing a watering system is whether or not to use a rain barrel. This collects rainwater, which you can then connect to your hose or irrigation system to water your garden. It is environmentally sound and efficient, but it is impractical in areas with little rainfall.

Finally, if you don't have the space to dig a plot or build a raised bed, you can garden in pots made of natural or recycled materials. Even if you have a backyard garden plot, pots are an excellent way to grow vegetables and herbs that are sensitive to excessive light and heat or have a tendency to take over spaces where they are planted.

Tender herbs, such as parsley and chives, are sensitive to heat in the summer, but if grown in pots, they can be moved to shadier areas during the day. And keep in mind that mint, which is delicious when freshly grown and comes in a dizzying array of flavors (chocolate, lemon, lime, pineapple, to name a few)—will not last long.

Soil as Plant Food

Now that you've chosen a location for your garden, the focus shifts to the soil, which is essential for growing a healthy and vibrant garden. The importance of composting in organic gardening cannot be overstated. It is not only the most effective method for improving and enriching your soil, but it is also environmentally friendly and cost-effective.

Obviously, in your first year of gardening, you'll need to provide some topsoil, either from your own backyard or from a garden supply store. You may eventually produce enough compost to replenish your soil each year while adding organic fertilizers as needed, but first, lay a solid foundation. Purchase topsoil from a reputable local supplier or a garden center that sells organic potting soil. Then, add your compost and begin.

Composting is the process of converting organic matter (grass, leaves, food waste) into a type of fertilizer. The goal is to achieve a balance of specific elements that promote plant growth while discouraging pests and disease in some cases. Compositing, in essence, requires time, some management, and a conscientious approach to reusing materials.

Again, there are numerous composters on the market, many of which are reasonably priced. Some of these for-sale models have the advantage of reducing the time required to produce usable compost. Compost must have a suitable time and enough internal heat to break down before it can be useful to your soil; thus, for first-time gardeners who want to compost on their own, you must either start composting about a year before you plan to garden (or less with some composting models: carefully research manufacturer's claims) or buy your compost from a reputable source.

Composting can truly be inexpensive and simple for the do-it-yourself gardener. It simply requires an out-of-the-way location— Naturally, composting emits some odor while working and can attract bugs—some basic materials and patience are required. I built my own composting system out of rebar, chicken wire, and dark plastic sheeting: I planted the rebar firmly into the ground in a wide circle (about the size of a backyard garbage can), wrapped it in chicken wire, and covered the wire in dark material (recycled plastic works well).

The dark covering traps heat and promotes aerobic breakdown of the material you put in the composter, while the chicken wire allows adequate oxygen and moisture levels to pass through. While not strictly necessary, a nice covering—I used an untreated round of cedar wood with a rope loop for a handle—can help to speed up the process and reduce odor.

What to put in your composter is straightforward, but it does necessitate some thought. Lawn cuttings can be composted, but be careful not to overburden your compost with cuttings from each mowing throughout the year. Take note of whether the grass you're composting has been treated with petrochemicals like fertilizer or herbicides.

Raking leaves from the yard near the end of the growing season is an excellent source of compost, but keep in mind what chemicals the trees in your area may have been treated with. Of course, food scraps are essential for nitrogen-rich composting: vegetable scraps, fruit peels, coffee grounds (and filters, if organically produced), egg shells, and so on. Avoid meat and dairy products, which take much longer to digest and can attract a variety of pests.

The ideal ratio is to mix "green" compost (food scraps, grass clippings, and the like) with "brown" compost (leaves, newspaper, untreated cardboard). A 1:3 ratio (one part green compost to three parts brown compost) is ideal, but it isn't necessary to be exact. Green compost basically heats things up, producing nitrogen and protein, whereas brown compost adds bulk and carbon to your compost while reducing odor.

I strongly recommend having a kitchen top composter to throw in your scraps while cooking and then transfer once or twice a week to your outdoor unit: this convenient setup ensures you keep your composter full and your outdoor unit clean. The trash can is nearly empty. These units are reasonably priced and can be found in a variety of garden stores as well as online.

How Does One Know When Composting Is Complete?
Essentially, it should be broken down by half, look like topsoil with few if any individual particles visible, and have lost any odor other than an earthy soil smell. When mixing in your compost at the start of the growing season, work from the bottom up, leaving behind whatever top layer has accumulated in the previous few months. Again, some commercial composters do not require you to do this.

While compost is the most important component of your topsoil, other organic fertilizers, such as manure and certain meals, can help your garden's health and growth potential. Manure is the most common garden addition, and it is considered a complete fertilizer with a high organic matter content. Using fresh manure in your garden during the growing season can contaminate plants and cause illness in anyone who consumes them.

Organic bone meal and blood meal can also be used to boost the potential of your soil: bone meal contains calcium and phosphate and promotes strong root health, whereas blood meal is high in nitrogen and promotes leaf growth (though too much can burn plant roots, so apply judiciously). There are also fish and seaweed-based meals and garden emulsions. Personally, I can attest to the effectiveness of fish skeletons: after a particularly successful fishing season, I will freeze my fish scraps until the end of the growing season, then simply till them into the soil before overwintering (even throwing in some past-their-prime whole carcasses). This technique has resulted in some of my most lush gardens.

Finally, getting your soil tested is an option to consider when starting an organic garden. The pH of your soil can help you determine which organic fertilizers to use and how much compost to add. This can be done at an extension center (see Chapter 1) or at local gardening stores; home testing kits are also becoming more widely available. This test will tell you whether your soil is acidic or alkaline.

Most plants prefer soil that is slightly acidic, with a pH of around 6.5. (7 is considered neutral). The most important nutrients, such as nitrogen and potassium, are most available to plants at this level. Lime is typically used to treat acidic soils, whereas sulfur is used to treat alkaline soils. This is where an extension center comes in handy, as their testing can pinpoint exactly what nutrients your soil is deficient in and/or overly abundant in. As a result, you can amend your soil with more or less of whatever specific nutrient you require, with different plants requiring different amounts, as discussed in the following chapter.

Planting Success Seeds

Seeds can be obtained from a variety of sources, including seed catalogs, local farms, and seed saving. When attempting to garden organically, keep in mind that the seeds themselves must come from an organic source; this does not preclude the use of hybrids, but it does prohibit the use of genetically modified seeds. GMO seeds are generally not a problem for home gardeners because they are limited to large industrial crops like corn and canola, but it never hurts to check. Some tomato varieties, such as Flavr Savr, are GMO products, and the FDA recently approved GMO potatoes for sale.

The most important decision for the home gardener, however, will be whether to use heirloom varieties (older varieties passed down through generations) or hybridized seeds. Heirloom varieties are wonderful and can broaden our understanding of what certain vegetables taste like, but they can be difficult to grow if they are not native to your area. Hybridized varieties are typically more hardy, but they can be less appealing than heirlooms. I would recommend sourcing some of both for the first-time gardener to ensure maximum harvest while providing a valuable learning experience.

To clarify, GMO seeds are a high-tech, relatively new innovation in creating almost entirely new plants, whereas hybridized seeds are a centuries-old tradition of selective cross-breeding of similar plants to produce a heartier version. To maximize the best qualities of each strain, hybridized seeds cross different strains of the same plant. Thus, a hybridized plant can be created by combining two strains, one that has proven to be particularly abundant and one that has proven to be particularly disease-resistant; the hybridized plant that results from this combination thrives and survives well.

For centuries, hybrids have been bred to meet human needs: the corn we know today is the result of thousands of years of hybridization, selecting for the plant that produced the largest ears; corn is a grass plant, and early corn produced tiny, tough ears.

We now have large ears of corn with juicy, ready-to-eat kernels as a result of crossing strains over time. The disadvantage of using hybridized seeds is that they do not always reproduce in the same way each season; for example, if you save seeds from a hybridized plant to use the following season, these may or may not produce the desired qualities derived from the hybrid plant. So, while purchasing seeds each year is not required, it is recommended to achieve the same results in a hybridized strain.

GMO seeds were genetically engineered in a laboratory, produced quickly through technological means, and did not undergo years of selective breeding. Because these seeds have only been widely used since the early 1990s, little is known about the environmental consequences of introducing these seeds and plants into the biome. GMO seeds are not limited to cross-breeding within their plant family, and as a result, science has created seeds that are genetically engineered to contain bacteria and, in some cases, viruses in addition to the original plant matter.

While supporters of GMO products point to their success in creating a more stable food supply, allowing more people to have food security, detractors point out that the unintended consequences of such genetic engineering have yet to be measured in terms of environmental stability and human health.

There are numerous examples of third-world countries rejecting genetically modified products (for example, "Golden Rice") as an extension of colonial domination, relegating local populations to the status of unwitting guinea pigs. While the European Union has kept a closer eye on the use of GMOs in its food supply than the United States, the National Organic Program has declared GMOs in organically labeled food to be unacceptable.

Heirloom seed is another type of seed to consider when growing an organic garden at home: these are traditional seed varieties that have been passed down through generations with little to no manipulation. Most heirloom plants are grown from seeds that have been around for at least 50 years.

Regarded as the pinnacle of Heirloom seeds and organic gardening are excitingly refreshing, diverse, and somewhat difficult to grow. When selecting heirloom seeds, look for varietals that have been commonly cultivated in your area; this means they will be adapted to the local climate and will have some natural defenses against local pests and diseases. Cherokee Purple tomatoes, for example, grow well in my area, but I've heard they're difficult to grow further north. These open-pollinators are the best plants to use if you want to save seeds for the following gardening season.

Seed Savers Exchange, Eden Brothers Heirloom Seeds, Johnny's Selected Seeds, Southern Exposure Seed Exchange, and the ubiquitous Burpee Seeds are some popular seed catalogs to investigate (which includes a section on heirlooms). Once you've established your garden, seed saving is an extremely cost-effective and environmentally friendly method of replenishing your garden for the following year.

There are many places to order seed saving kits, but the process is simple enough to do at home with a few old, empty spice jars or paper envelopes. Make sure your seeds are dry and debris-free before storing them in a cool, dry place for next season. The Seed Savers Exchange website has a wealth of information on how to save seeds, as well as recommendations on which seeds are most practical for the average home gardener to save (some plants require more effort than others to grow from saved seeds; reliable ones to save include bean and tomato seeds).

Now that you have your seeds, the best way to use them—direct seeding or seeding and transplanting—depends on what and where you are growing. It is often more practical for the home gardener to use a combination of direct seeding and transplanting, either by purchasing seedlings or fostering them at home. It takes a dedicated gardener to put in the time and effort required to start seedlings from seed and transplant later in the season, so consider how much time you are willing to devote.

Many seeds can and should be sown directly into the garden, and while this is technically possible, it is not recommended. While any plant can be grown from seed in soil, using seedlings makes more sense for the home gardener in many cases.

Direct seeding is the practice of planting seeds directly into prepared garden soil. This method is ideal for delicate plants that do not tolerate transplanting, such as lettuces and greens. Seed packets will usually include instructions on how deep to plant and how far apart to space seeds, which should be followed.

When it comes to the tiny lettuce seeds, however, don't worry too much about spacing; it's inevitable that you'll accidentally drop more than one seed right next to each other in your shallow row. Simply begin separating plants and thinning your lettuce patch once they've grown to a height suitable for harvesting some bay leaves. Make sure to pull the plant up by its roots to allow room for its neighbor to grow. Consume the baby lettuces right away and compost the roots. Many lettuce and greens varieties (kale, collards,

Swiss chard) allow you to cut leaves to use, leaving roots in the ground so leaves grow back, at least two or three times before the lettuce becomes too strong or bitter. At that point, simply pull up the roots and compost them, or leave them to go to seed if you have the patience to harvest the minute seeds.

Plants with climbing vines, such as sugar snap peas and pole beans, can also be seeded directly. Plant these alongside your fence to encourage vines to grow into the mesh or wires. However, be wary of vines snaking into other areas of your garden; you may need to build an internal barrier to keep the vines in check.

Tomatoes are technically vines, though most have thicker "trunks" and grow like haphazard bushes. When a tomato plant gets a foot or so off the ground, the best way to tame it is to wrap it in a tomato cage. Otherwise, you'll end up with tomato vines lying on the ground, causing the fruit to rot or remaining unripe in the absence of direct sunlight.

The climate is another factor to consider when deciding whether to direct seed or use transplants. Some plants will survive a hard freeze many require it to thrive—but many will not. Thus, Seedlings grown in greenhouses or indoors are an excellent way to get a head start on the growing season, especially if you live in a colder climate, and a convenient way to plan your garden space with a clear visual representation of what will sprout up where.

For lettuce, greens, and beans, for example, I direct seed, and for tomatoes, chiles, and herbs, I use transplanted seedlings. Of course, root vegetables are difficult to transplant without disturbing or destroying the edible root itself. The following chapter discusses in detail some specific vegetables and herbs that are well-suited for the organic home garden, as well as some advice on how to treat each.

Chapter Three

VEGETABLE VICTORY: CHOOSING THE BEST PLANTS FOR THE GARDEN

In addition to deciding which plants to grow, this chapter should teach you how to make the most of your garden space and how to use companion planting. This is the age-old notion that certain plants grown together to nurture each other by attracting beneficial insects and repelling pests while also providing nutrients and/or other types of support.

Before I get into the list (and to avoid endless arguments at the dinner table), I should clarify that I am characterizing some plants that are technically fruits—tomatoes, cucumbers, chiles—as suitable for a vegetable garden, as well as including herbs. Even the most oblivious gardening expert will admit that any home garden worth its salt will have some, if not all, of these intruders.

Finally, this list provides a high-level overview of each plant. When and how you plant will be determined by the zone you live in and the type of garden you intend to cultivate. Some general guidelines are provided; consult with local sources for specifics on how to get each plant you choose to thrive in your organic garden. For ideas on how to use your plants in the kitchen, see Chapter 5.

Herbs

Herbs are nearly as essential to the home cook as salt and pepper and are among the easiest and arguably some of the most useful plants to cultivate in your garden. Herbs can also be grown in pots, freeing up space in your raised bed for other plants (if using a drip irrigation system, pots are fairly easy to integrate with spot watering emitters).

During the growing season, it is undeniably satisfying to simply pop outside and scissor off a small handful of herbs to enhance any meal. And, depending on where you live, many herbs will return each year and be among the first pleasures to be harvested at the start of the next spring.

Herbs can be grown from seed or directly seeded into your garden, though herb seeds are typically so small that they are difficult to handle. I prefer to get seedlings from a trusted local source that uses organic methods. Plant seedlings of annual herbs after the last frost.

Parsley

True workhorse of the garden—and the kitchen—parsley is more than just a garnish; it can be a key ingredient in salads and fresh sauces. My favorite is Italian flat-leaf parsley; it has a stronger flavor than curly parsley and its broad, flat leaves are more appealing in many applications.

Parsley can withstand direct sunlight, but it is not as hardy as basil. If you live in a hot climate, plant in a pot that can be moved to a shaded area when it gets too hot. It takes two to three months to mature. If your area does not have harsh winters, parsley may return, but only for another year.

Basil

Another garden wonder, Genovese basil is a wonderfully hearty, generous plant that grows to be about two feet tall when fully mature. I've also grown globe basil and purple (Thai) basil, both of which are delicious, though Genovese is the most "all-purpose" variety. For best results, plant in a garden bed. There are many other heirloom basil varieties, but Genovese is one of the strongest and most productive. It takes about three months to reach full potential, but it can be clipped carefully throughout the season.

Basil prefers full sun—and does NOT like cold, so don't clip and store in the refrigerator, as it will wilt and turn black quickly—and to keep your plant from bolting, trim back the flowers that appear during the season. Many instructions will say to "pinch" off flowers, but the rough action of pinching can allow disease to penetrate deeper into the plant. Cutting is always better for you.

Chives

Chives, one of the first signs of spring, will produce for several years before needing to be replanted. As a result, I keep chives in pots so that when it comes time to till my garden plot for the new spring season, I don't have to worry about digging them up. Don't limit yourself to delicate "onion-y" chives; the stronger flavor of garlic chives is fantastic in a variety of Asian and other dishes.

Chives thrive in most climates and require little care to thrive. When they flower, don't throw away the chive blossoms; they make a tasty garnish, or if you have a lot of them, soak them in vinegar for a few days to make flavored vinegar for salad dressings.

Mint

I've grown numerous varieties of mint over the years—spearmint, peppermint, lime mint, chocolate mint, and Corsican mint—and have only sabotaged one plant once by attempting to plant it in a frustratingly wet part of the yard. Even mint succumbed to the onslaught of water. As previously stated, mint can quickly take over a garden, so keep your mint plants in pots.

Mint, like chives, will be one of the first plants to emerge in early spring. It will return for several years, and, like basil, mint does not like being stored in the fridge. If you clipped a little more than you wanted, put the remainder in a water glass with a little water and set it on the counter for a day or two.

Tarragon

Tarragon is an underutilized herb in American cooking, with a lovely anise-like flavor. It's delicious stuffed into a chicken with lemon and garlic, as well as roasted, and making tarragon vinegar is a seasonal treat in my house.

Tarragon also prefers full sun, making it an excellent choice for garden planting. It prefers to grow close to the ground and spread out, so give it some space. Unlike basil and chives, this herb dries well, so make sure to save it before winter arrives.

Oregano

I almost always have oregano on hand for Italian and Mexican cooking. It is impossible to purchase fresh or dried oregano that compares to what you can grow in your own garden (though, arguably, that could be said of most herbs). This is another low-growing plant that, while not as large as tarragon, requires at least 10" of space to thrive. Plant this in your bed with basil and tarragon. Because it hugs the ground, it is prone to overwatering.

Other Plants

There are many other herbs that I have grown organically with great success; the ones listed above are simply the ones I prefer to keep on hand at all times. If you like dill, it is a natural pest repellent and would be an excellent addition to your garden bed. Of course, don't forget cilantro (which I don't plant but love because there's only so much space in the garden and cilantro is cheap at my local market). Sage, rosemary, and thyme are all excellent drying plants at the end of the season. Some herbs are less common, such as lemon verbena (delicious but aggressive in the garden, like mint), lavender (as pretty as it is fragrant), and lovage (a celery-flavored herb).

Vegetables

The beautiful crop of multicolored, delicious, and nutritious vegetables that you coax out of your lovingly tended soil will undoubtedly be the crowning achievement of any home garden, and the envy of every neighbor. The following are just a few ideas, chosen because they thrive in organic gardens and are, for the most part, relatively easy to care for. I also tried to include representative vegetables for each season, so you can practice succession planting if you want, ensuring a continuous crop of homegrown, organic produce all year. More information on succession planting can be found in Chapter 7.

Lettuces

Direct seed in early spring for tender greens that will last all spring and early summer. Because most lettuces dislike extreme heat, make room in your garden for other plants this summer. Replant lettuces for a later harvest as your summer crops begin to fade in the fall. As mentioned in the previous chapter, with lettuce, don't worry about putting a single seed in a single hole; instead, carve out a shallow trough and sprinkle seeds down the length of it. Thin your crop as needed once it begins to leaf out; use the baby lettuces in salads in the early spring. Crisphead lettuces are the heartiest and least susceptible to pests, making them ideal for the first-time gardener. But don't be afraid to experiment with looseleaf, butterhead, and romaine lettuce varieties. Most lettuces will produce at least two nice heads, if not three: to get a second or third harvest, cut the leaves near the base of the plant rather than pulling up by the roots.

Greens

Other spring-loving green plants include spinach, arugula, Swiss chard, and various Asian greens (mizuna, gai lan, bok choy). Direct seed in early spring, and these greens, like lettuce, will continue to produce until the heat of summer arrives. These plants can also be grown in the early fall, though I prefer hearty kale and collard greens at that time of year, as well as savoyed spinach, which can produce throughout the winter. All of these greens thrive in cooler weather, but they require direct sunlight and plenty of water. Be warned: insects enjoy eating lettuce and leafy greens just as much as we do. Expect to lose a little due to bugs. More information on pest control can be found in Chapter 4.

Peas, Sugar Snap

I gardened for many years before taking a chance on sugar snap peas (and pole beans), thinking that their vine-y needs would be too much trouble. They turn out to be simple to grow (especially if you've worked with tomato plants before) and will climb whatever trellis you set up for them. In early spring, direct seed in a corner of your garden where you've cordoned off a section (say, about 2' in from the garden's border) with chicken wire or recycled plastic fencing.

Pea tendrils require something to grab onto, which prevents them from latching onto other plants. These are among the first spring vegetables to mature. Other peas, such as English peas or snow peas, can also be grown in this manner; I just like the convenience (no shelling!) and flavor of the sugar snap. Pole beans begin to produce once the sugar snaps are finished.

Radishes

Radishes, another early spring crop, grow quickly and mature in about a month. Plant directly in the garden (as with root vegetables, transplanting does not work well). Depending on your climate, you should be able to grow two or three rounds of radishes before the weather gets too hot. Radishes thrive in temperatures that do not exceed 70 degrees. For best results, keep the soil moist. Tender and mild French breakfast radishes are a favorite of mine, and Easter egg radishes produce lovely pink, purple, and red bouquets.

Cruciferous Veggies

The most common cruciferous vegetables found in markets and gardens are cabbage, broccoli, cauliflower, and Brussels sprouts. Broccoli and cabbage are the easiest to grow, while cauliflower is the most fickle. These are early spring and fall crops, similar to lettuces and greens (Brussel sprouts are the last to harvest at the end of the fall). You must have enough space in your garden plot to grow a nice row or two to make a harvest worthwhile. These are also best when seeded directly.

Bean Poles

Similar to peas, these are the simplest beans to grow (see above for more details on where to plant). They only need a trellis and some time to produce a satisfying harvest. Because these are harvested later in the season, you can direct sow these after your sugar snaps are finished for the season in early summer if space is limited; your trellis will already be in place and ready for climbing. However, if your climate is extremely hot in the early summer, the beans may not produce much. I particularly like Provider beans because they are prolific producers. Harvest frequently to promote more growth. Growing beans to dry is a completely different matter, and one that is out of most home gardeners' reach.

Okra

This plant is extremely prolific and thrives in hot, humid climates, though it can be grown almost anywhere with direct sunlight. Transplant in late spring and only grow as many plants as you think you'll need; in my area, gardeners are hard pressed to give it away at the height of summer due to the abundance of okra. Also, once the plants begin to produce, keep a close eye on them. Okra is at its best when it is about the length of a pinky finger, and it can nearly double in size in a day.

Tomatoes

When you compare a homegrown tomato to a supermarket tomato, you'll understand why I started gardening in the first place. While all produce tastes better fresh from the ground and organically grown, tomatoes in particular highlight the wonders of home gardening (and the horrors of what industrial agriculture has done to this beloved fruit). There are so many tomato varieties that there is one that can be grown in almost any location.

In late winter/early spring, direct seed these plants indoors for transplanting after the last frost. In my Zone 7 area, I usually wait until after tax day to plant seedlings. Indoor seedling care is time-consuming but cost-effective if you plan on growing a large number of tomato plants. Because I only grow six or seven plants per season, I prefer to get my seedlings locally from an organic producer.

Tomatoes require direct sunlight and plenty of water throughout the growing season. Tomatoes in my garden begin to produce in earnest in July (I usually get lucky with a couple at the end of June) and continue until October, with the exception of drought years with 100+ degree temperatures. Set up a tomato cage around each plant once the seedlings have sprouted and begun to thrive. Give your tomato plants plenty of room to grow, and check on them on a regular basis once they begin to grow quickly and produce, gently taming the vines through the cage.

Tomato vines will always begin to look a little wild at the height of the growing season, so don't be concerned as long as they are healthy. Also, be wary of avian threats from above: the first year I planted tomato seedlings, I left them alone for a few hours while I cooked dinner. When I went to check on them that evening, the birds had stripped every single plant of its leaves!

Most survived, but to prevent such an apocalypse, I've strung a makeshift net around the perimeter of the garden—make sure the netting is suspended so it doesn't suffocate the plants. Almost everyone, from birds and bugs to roving neighborhood kids, love tomatoes? See Chapter 4 for some advice on everything except the neighborhood kids.

I like to grow cherry or grape tomatoes (my favorites are Black Cherry and Yellow Pear) in a large pot near the garden because these smaller plants don't require as much space and often don't require cages. They also mature faster, and by mid-summer, they are ready to pick off the vine and toss into a salad.

For other varieties, I rely on heirloom tomatoes native to my area, such as Arkansas Travelers, Cherokee Purples, and Royal Hillbilly tomatoes (a rarer heirloom definitely worth seeking out); check with your local farmers' market or gardening store to see what varietals are native to your area. Brandywine and Green Zebra are two other well-known heirlooms (this one remains green when ripe). If you want to can tomatoes, paste tomatoes work best, with San Marzano being the standard-bearer. Visit Chapters 5 and 6 for many ideas on how to use and preserve these treasures.

Cucumbers

Cucumbers, another prolific vine-like plant, thrive in most warm climates. Because they are so prolific and their vines grow so freely, I recommend making another small bed for them (which can also be used for larger squash varieties and/or melons) or, at the very least, cordoning off a section of the garden to limit vine expansion within the rest of your bed.

Cucumbers come in a wide range of varieties, from traditional slicing and pickling cucumbers to Asian varieties with fewer seeds. For a long time, I didn't bother with cucumbers—they're cheap and plentiful in the supermarket, albeit grown industrially and frequently coated in wax—until I discovered the Armenian cucumber: these pale varietals produce large, long fruit with small seed pods and a clean, crisp flavor that reminds you that cucumbers are closely related to melons.

They produce so well (and don't turn bitter even when large) that I supplied a local restaurant from my small patch for a couple of years. One large Armenian cucumber can serve as a side dish for a table of six to eight people. Direct seed in the garden in the spring in a sunny spot; most cucumber varieties thrive through the hot summer and into early fall. If you grow cucumbers (or tomatoes or melons) and have sensitive skin, I recommend wearing long sleeves or long gloves when weeding and harvesting among these vines. If I don't cover my skin when rooting through cucumber vines, I'll itch for two days.

Melons

Melons, another low-growing vine, can be prolific if given enough space and the right varietal for your climate. Because of space constraints, most backyard gardeners cannot grow the familiar melon crops of watermelon, honeydew, and cantaloupe. If you want to grow some—and growing melons organically produces beautiful, pure-tasting fruit (a melon is essentially a water filtration system)—look into some lesser-known, smaller varieties like Chanterais melons.

When fully mature, they fit in the palm of your hand and taste like a sweeter cantaloupe. They aren't as easy to grow everywhere—too much or too little water will stymie their growth—but with some care, these are tasty treats to harvest all summer. Plant in the same manner as cucumbers (above).

Other Peppers and Chile

Chile and bell peppers are colorful and tasty garden additions. They are also, for the most part, hearty and thrive in warm climates. Of course, the larger the pepper, the more space it will require; otherwise, most pepper varieties can be planted in spring and harvested throughout the summer and early fall. I've had success with common peppers such as jalapeos, serranos, Anaheims, and poblanos.

I've also grown padrons, which are lovely Spanish peppers that can be sautéed in olive oil and eaten whole (the fun is in the surprise: most are sweet and mild, but one or two will pack a spicy punch); shishitos, a Japanese pepper treated similarly to padrons; habaneros, the super spicy brilliant orange pepper; Bolivian rainbow peppers, which are more of an ornamental plant with their purple, red, and orange bouquets of small peppers; Grinding your own cayenne powder will forever turn you off the dusty supermarket stuff. Most peppers are simple to grow IF you have a long summer.

Squash and similar vegetables

Squash, like okra, can outperform in hot climates, but their easygoing presence ensures garden success. Again, squash varieties require space to spread out and thrive, so make sure you have enough. Direct seed in the spring for a late summer bounty. Try zucchini, yellow crook-necked squash, and patty pan varieties, which thrive in most areas with a long summer.

Acorn and butternut squash varieties mature later and grow larger. As a result, they are ideal for harvesting in the fall. They do, however, require more space and time. In addition, eggplant, a nightshade plant, has a similar growing capacity and timing to squash.

Alliums (Garlic & Onions & Leeks)

Garlic and onions are excellent crops to grow in a small garden if you follow succession planting: these are typically overwintered, so you plant in late fall for a harvest the following spring or early summer, freeing up space for later plantings during the growing season. There are many places to get garlic and onion bulbs, and you'll be surprised at the incredible variety: Filaree Garlic Farms has an excellent selection of organic, heirloom bulb varieties, and I've successfully grown more than a dozen different types of garlic and shallots (Filaree Farms also has a selection of potato seeds and other plants).

'If you don't want to deal with exotic varieties, you can simply buy a head of garlic and plant the bulbs in your garden, root end down. Budget-friendly, if not guaranteed heirloom. I plant in mid-to late October and harvest in early June in my area. I usually plant 50 or 60 bulbs because garlic, like onions and shallots, can be stored properly until the following growing season.

Because leeks grow in both the spring and fall, you can plant seeds in late summer (after you've harvested your garlic and shallots, for example) and they'll mature over the fall and winter. Pluck them in the spring to be replaced by new seedlings. The allium family is a great way to create a year-round garden experience.

Potatoes

This is another crop that requires a lot of space to be profitable, but if you have it, the sheer variety of potatoes available, combined with their long shelf life, makes for an exciting crop. Potatoes thrive in cool soil, so plan your planting so that you can harvest before the heat of summer sets in. Some varieties overwinter well, while others can be planted in early spring and harvested in early summer. My grandparents grew potatoes by removing the eyes from older, withered potatoes and planting them; for more certain results, obtain seed potatoes from a reputable grower (Filaree Garlic Farms or Seed Savers Exchange are reliable online sources).

SOME UNUSUAL CONSIDERATIONS

All of the crops listed above are suitable for organic gardening and allow you to space your planting throughout the year to make the best use of your garden space. There are a plethora of other vegetables and fruits to consider as well. The crops listed above are ones with which I am familiar and, for the most part, are simple to grow.

Other crops I enjoy, such as asparagus and berries in general, I buy at farmers' markets rather than growing myself because they are either temperamental or so tasty to pests that I can't keep up with them. Artichokes are another crop I've tried and failed to grow because it's just too hot where I live; there are some excellent heirloom varieties out there just waiting for you to discover.

Furthermore, the gardening world is whatever you make of it. You are only limited by your location, and even then, you can sometimes exert some control over nature by planting in a greenhouse or hoop house. Some seasons, I've indulged in the slightly more time-consuming practice of moving plants from outdoors to indoors to outdoors: a small kumquat tree that thrived for several years by being protected from winter; a bay leaf tree that produces a continuous supply of leaves (fresh bay leaves are astonishingly fragrant); and many ornamental plants, some of which I've had for more than a decade. In our technologically saturated age, gardening in any form is a rare pleasure. Take a risk and get your hands dirty in a positive way!

Planting Companion Plants

This is the practice of planting specific groups of plants together in order to benefit from their mutually beneficial properties. These characteristics include complementary nutrient requirements, pest repellent abilities, and/or growth habits. Companion planting has long been used in many cultures, the received wisdom of hundreds of generations of farmers who have learned what works well together through trial and error.

Prior to the advent of industrial agriculture, farmers could rely on companion planting to ensure adequate harvests. Consider Native American cultures, where maize (corn), beans, and squash are commonly planted: the tall maize plants shade the low-growing squash while providing a natural trellis for the climbing beans; in turn, the prickly vines of the squash discourage pests, and the nitrogen-rich beans provide soil nutrients. Any backyard plot can benefit from some variation of this ancient wisdom.

Herbs are excellent natural pest repellents: for example, strongly scented herbs like basil and dill are excellent companions for tomatoes, keeping hornworms at bay. Rosemary, sage, and mint can deter moths that eat greens.

Other herbs attract beneficial insects like ladybugs, which eat leaf-destroying aphids (parsley is good for this). Many gardeners swear by marigolds, which protect roots by repelling harmful worms. Earthworms are excellent garden companions, but there are a variety of nematodes that thrive on plant roots rather than soil.

Shade is essential for certain plants: leafy greens require some shade if they are to last into late spring or early summer, so taller plants can act as a sun shield. Space can also be a common sense result of companion planting wisdom: planting lower growing herbs like tarragon, oregano, and rosemary in between tomato plants gives you more space.

Allowing vines to spread while also providing pest protection Furthermore, another sub-category of companion planting—planting continuously throughout the year (see examples above)—has the added benefit of discouraging weed growth.

Nutrient swapping benefits a variety of companion plants while also improving soil quality. Nitrogen-rich plants, such as peas or beans (or cover crops: see Chapter 7) replenish your soil with nitrogen, which tomatoes require.

Seasonality is a good rule of thumb to follow when it comes to companion planting: for example, radishes and greens grow well together because they both like cool temperatures and well-drained soil; tomatoes and squash grow well together because they both like lots of sun and do well in heat, and peppers grow well together because they both like lots of sun and provide some natural pest repellent.

These are just a few examples of the vast amount of information available on the benefits and techniques of companion planting. Farmer's Almanacs, farmers' markets, and cooperative extension services are all great places to get more information on how to set up your garden for success.

Chapter Four

PEST PREPARATION: EMBRACE THE INEVITABLE

The first organic gardening rule I learned after attending a seminar at my local cooperative extension service was straightforward: "one for me, one for the pests." It can be frustrating to begin organic gardening, especially if you have previously used traditional petrochemical fertilizers (MiracleGro) and pesticides (Sevin Dust) as quick fixes. It can be heartbreaking to discover a gnawed leaf or a wormy tomato after all the time and effort you put into creating your beautiful garden.

However, I would strongly argue that the short-term benefits of petrochemical fertilizers and pesticides are not worth it in the long run: the effects on soil health, potential groundwater contamination, the ethical quandary of sourcing petroleum-based products, not to mention the proven health risks posed to humans, far outweigh the perceived benefit of producing more unblemished produce. Furthermore, organic gardening attracts beneficial critters such as ladybugs and earthworms, whereas the use of petrochemicals indiscriminately destroys your microbiome. Accepting the inevitable does not imply defeat; rather, it means embracing the thriving biological community that you have worked so hard to foster and nurture.

Having said that, we'd all prefer to eat more of our products rather than leave them to pests. See the list below for some suggestions on how to manage your potential pest population. I don't bother addressing herbicides because they have no place in a backyard garden. Fertilizer is covered in Chapter 2.

ORGANIC PESTICIDES

There are many high-quality organic pesticides on the market today, as the demand for purer products has grown over the last two decades. If you decide to buy these products commercially, look for the OMRI seal, which indicates that the product has been vetted by the Organic Materials Review Institute, a non-profit organization that works under the NOP (USDA's National Organic Program). This seal should give you confidence that the product meets the highest government standards.

If you want to avoid using commercial pesticides, there are a variety of pesticides that you can make at home using common household ingredients. Stock up on spray bottles for convenience.

Native farmers have used neem oil for centuries because of its overall effectiveness in repelling pests. The neem plant's juice has been shown to contain fifty or more natural pesticides. Organic neem oil is widely available in garden stores and online. Combine half an ounce with a teaspoon of organic liquid soap in two quarts of warm water. It loses effectiveness after a few days, so use it within a day or two.

Mineral oil is also a good pesticide because it dehydrates insect eggs. 20 milliliters of high-quality mineral oil in a liter of warm water

Citrus oil combined with cayenne pepper is especially effective against ants. Many natural food stores and online retailers sell essential citrus oil. In a cup of warm water, combine a few drops of essential oil (about ten) and a teaspoon of cayenne pepper. Use right away. Another application for citrus oil is to combine one ounce of orange essential oil and three tablespoons of organic liquid soap in a gallon of water. This appears to be effective on slugs.

Eucalyptus oil repels wasps and flies (though it also deters bees, which you might want around). Simply sprinkling a few drops around the area where you've seen wasps or flies will keep them away.

Spider mites can be easily and effectively removed with salt spray. Spray a gallon of water with a couple of tablespoons of coarse salt (some recommend Himalayan salt in particular), then spray directly onto affected plants.

Garlic and onion spray is a longer-lasting solution that can be refrigerated for several weeks. In a quart of warm water, combine a clove or two of organic garlic and a medium-sized organic onion. Allow for an hour or two before adding a teaspoon of cayenne pepper and a tablespoon of organic liquid soap. Remove solids before transferring to a spray bottle, but keep solids in any solution you store.

Other ideas include making a tea from chrysanthemum flowers and adding neem oil to boost effectiveness, making a tobacco spray by steeping loose tobacco in warm water overnight and mixing chile powder with diatomaceous earth and water. These are mentioned with reservations because the first two can be harmful to certain plants and the latter can suffocate delicate plants.

Other Natural Treatments

Organic gardeners quickly learn how to be creative in their pest control efforts. The above organic pesticide recipes are a good place to start, but there are other tricks and tips that gardeners share by word of mouth to help with specific problems. (Keep in mind that insects aren't the only creatures who might find your garden appealing.) The effectiveness of the following methods has not been rigorously tested; however, many of them are simple, common sense ideas that are easily implemented and arguably effective.

Coffee grounds and eggshells sprinkled around the base of a tomato plant will discourage hornworms from crawling across the prickly barrier and up to your vines and fruits. Other gardeners swear by encircling your seedling with an old coffee can with the bottom cut out; this works but can impede root growth.

Beer can also be used to attract critters such as slugs. Bury a beer container in the ground near your plants (or place a low saucer next to them); the bugs will crawl in but not emerge.

Diatomaceous earth is a natural substance made up of finely ground fossilized material that functions similarly to eggshells and coffee grounds. As with the aforementioned, this should be sprinkled only around affected plants to avoid disturbing the balance of your soil.

Handpicking slugs, snails, and hornworms off your plants is a low-tech, non-intrusive way to get rid of these pests if they happen to land on your plants. To kill the intruders, throw them into a bucket of brine. For best results, do this in the early morning when the slugs are active.

Vinegar can be easily used to repel small pests, particularly fruit flies (which should be called "vinegar" flies because they are attracted to the gases produced by vinegar).

The vinegar mimics the release of fruits, not the fruit itself). Spray lightly on pest areas for outdoor use; this can also be used on weeds, but be careful not to harm your own plants. Put vinegar in a small bowl next to your problem area—unrefrigerated produce or an indoor composter—and cover with plastic wrap punctured with toothpick-sized holes.

If you live in an area that attracts a variety of critters, from rabbits and possums to birds and neighborhood cats, netting is almost essential. Netting can be inconvenient at times and can trap butterflies, but it is usually worth it to save the garden from the raiding hordes. Cheesecloth can also be draped over plants to allow light and water to penetrate while keeping small pests and insects out. It is not as long-lasting as garden netting. To keep birds away, use foil strips in a scarecrow fashion. Change locations on a regular basis to keep them guessing.

Fake snakes have previously served as an effective deterrent to rabbits and birds for me. Change their location on a regular basis.

Mulch is an excellent way to keep your soil moist and temperature stable. Cedar and eucalyptus mulch are also said to repel pests because their strong scents repel many insects. Mulch can also help to keep weeds at bay during the growing season. If you aren't succession planting or using cover crops, you can use a mulch to protect your soil over the winter.

Disease Control

I've discovered that disease is more damaging to my gardens than pests and that many diseases are caused by poor soil health and simple maintenance techniques. Preventing disease is the best way to combat it, and there are several simple things you can do to avoid common garden problems.

Soil health is perhaps the most important step in disease prevention. See Chapter 2 for more information on soil preparation, but as a reminder, having your soil tested is one of the best things you can do before the main gardening season begins (or, indeed, at the end, so you can get a jump on next year's plans).

Check that the pH is correct (for most edible plants, it should be around 6.5) and that your soil nutrients are adequate. A lack of nitrogen in your soil inhibits or stunts growth, whereas a lack of calcium can result in the dreaded bottom-end rot in tomatoes. A variety of problems can be avoided by testing and correcting your soil regularly.

Proper maintenance is also simple but essential. Over-fertilizing a garden can promote disease, so use caution. Keep your equipment clean and get rid of old rusted tools, especially pruners, and use tools for pruning rather than pinching or tearing. The more ragged the stem is left after pruning or bobbing flowering shoots, the more susceptible the plant is to disease.

Most importantly, water in the morning so that plants have time to dry before nightfall; this helps to prevent fungal diseases, which are among the most common problems in home gardens. In the event of an unusually wet spring, keep an eye out for fungal diseases such as tomato blight. This will stunt and eventually kill your tomato plant if not addressed immediately.

Natural fungicides such as bicarbonates can be used to prevent blight, rot, and mildew. Although baking soda can be used, it is not as effective as bicarbonates containing ammonium or potassium. These are classified as non- Human toxicity Green Cure is a well-known fungicide that is widely available on the market.

Biological fungicides, such as Bacillus subtilis, are effective in combating many common garden diseases while causing no harm to humans or animals. While prevention is still preferable, biological fungicides can be effective in combating disease once it has spread. Copper and sulfur-based products can also be used for prevention, though they can be harmful to some plants and animals. As a result, these should be used with caution.

Products based on soil bacteria are used to protect roots and seeds while causing no harm to earthworms or other beneficial insects. If you've ever had issues with seeds rotting in the ground or roots failing to take hold, treat your garden with one of these products before planting, such as Mycostop or Root Shield.

Chapter Five

HEALTHY HARVEST: WEEDING, PRUNING, AND USING

While many aspects of preparation and maintenance have already been discussed throughout the book, the focus here is on what to do once your seedlings have sprouted and your garden has sprung. Following that are suggestions for what to do with your product, as well as some quick and easy recipe ideas for making the most of your healthy harvest.

Weeding Tips In General

Preparation and prevention are almost as important as execution in many great endeavors in life. That is, the best way to keep weeds under control in your garden is to prevent them from growing in the first place. To begin, use a raised bed of some kind; this discourages weed growth by placing a healthy layer of topsoil over your subsoil.

Second, create a barrier between your garden's subsoil and topsoil to prevent weeds from sprouting from the subsoil (good soil, compost, and manure if used). The barriers can be made of anything that isn't chemically treated (which would be harmful to soil, groundwater, and plants while also diminishing your proudly organic brand): old cardboard, a thick layer of newspapers, and biodegradable fabric will all work to varying degrees.

Furthermore, using a drip irrigation system is beneficial: because the irrigation system is more specifically directed at the plants you want to grow, it does not encourage grass seeds to grow randomly. Smart planting will also help to reduce weed growth: while you should avoid crowding your plants, close planting of desired crops leaves little room for weeds.

However, keep in mind that no amount of preparation can prevent ALL weed growth. Weeds will inevitably grow in your garden. Your priority should be to keep weed growth to a minimum, allowing more room and nutrients for your desired plants to grow. So, when the inevitable weeds appear, there are other options for bringing them in and keeping them under control.

Mulching your garden is always an effective weed barrier; additionally, it regulates the temperature of your topsoil, keeping it warm in cooler weather and protecting it from the direct heat of summer. Keep your mulch at a depth of about two inches, and be aware that some commercial mulches may contain chemicals and/or weed seeds. Make an informed decision.

Hand weeding will become necessary at some point during the growing season. Some simple weeding tips: weed in the dewy mornings or after a light rain, as wet soil more easily releases the weed root. Pull the weed up, root and all, or it will regrow quickly. If your weeds become tough or aggressive, use a small garden trowel to help pull them up without damaging nearby plant roots. Weed frequently! The longer the weed is allowed to grow in your soil, the more difficult it will be to remove.

Finally, while it is unclear why this is the case, most horticulturists will agree that organic gardens with plenty of good compost simply don't sprout as many weeds. A healthy garden starts with healthy soil.

Pruning Guidelines In General

While pruning is not the most important concern for a vegetable garden—harvesting is—there are some simple tips you can use for your entire backyard to keep it looking good and growing well. If you have perennials in your garden, such as mint or chives, make sure to prune them back at the end of the growing season so that the dead material does not overmuch the soil and prevent new growth from sprouting the following season.

Also, prune any dead growth you see during the season (though keep in mind that "dead" growth on one of your plants during the season is often indicative of disease). Finally, during the growing season, be sure to top any flowering plants, such as basil and lettuces, to keep them producing and prevent them from going to seed.

What not to do in a vegetable garden when it comes to pruning may be even more important: no matter how tempting it may be to prune back vine-growing plants (tomatoes, cucumbers, squash, beans, peas), do not do it. While this type of pruning is occasionally beneficial, it often stunts the growth of fruits and vegetables and introduces disease.

How To Make The Most Of Your Harvest

Finally! After all of your hard work, hours, days, and months, you can finally enjoy the fruits of your labor. This is the most satisfying, rewarding, and even delicious aspect of gardening. Here are some basic tips for harvesting your plants and using them once they're happily lined up on your kitchen countertops. The following suggestions are not "recipes" in the traditional sense, with a precise list of ingredients and measurements, but rather methods of preparing specific dishes based on what you've harvested.

These methods are open to improvisation and substitution, so use your imagination!

Herbs

When harvesting herbs, the general rule of thumb is to harvest only what you need at the time (after all, that's why you have them in the backyard, right?). If you gather a little too enthusiastically, avoid the refrigerator and instead place the extra-cut herbs in a glass of water on a windowsill (or, alternately, use an herb arrangement as a centerpiece for your dinner table: lovely and practical). When gathering herbs, make sure to snip or cut them rather than pinching or pulling them, which can introduce disease.

Dishes Featuring Herbal Ingredients

Pesto is the first thing that comes to mind when thinking of fresh garden herbs. While it's not a stand-alone dish, it can be the star of the show when spooned over grilled steak or chops, swirled into soup, or stirred into a grain salad. A basic proportion of 2 cups herbs, 12 cup nuts, a couple of garlic cloves, some acidity (lemon, lime, orange, light vinegar) to taste, and 34 cup quality olive oil. Depending on what you're serving it with, you can add cheese, usually about 12 cup hard cheeses like parmesan or pecorino. Blend this in a food processor or blender, or if you have a good mortar and pestle, take your time grinding it together by hand. This latter, more traditional method yields a supremely creamy pesto.

While most people think of pesto in terms of the classic basil and pine nuts pairing, there are many other herb-nut combinations to consider: mint and walnuts, which are especially well-suited for spooning over lamb chops; parsley and pecans, which go well with steak; or chives/garlic chives and peanuts, which add an Asian flair. Consider arugula, a spicy green, for pesto; it's a hearty accompaniment to grilled meats or fish.

You can also use your herbal bounty to make a delicious salad. A lovely starter for any occasion is a mix of tender young herb leaves tossed with a light vinaigrette and topped with some delicate shavings of cheese or grated nuts. I like to combine 3 parts parsley and 1 part mint with a lemon-based vinaigrette of 1 part lemon to 2 parts oil, with a splash of Dijon mustard and honey for emulsification and balance.

If you have some smoked Spanish paprika (pimentón) on hand, it adds a touch of sweet heat, and salt to taste. Using a vegetable peeler, shave some hard cheese over the top, allowing it to curl nicely, and/or grate some toasted pecans or walnuts over the top. Beautiful, nutritious, and delectable!

Tabouli is yet another famously herb-forward salad dish. While many Americanized versions contain a lot of other ingredients — which is fine — the traditional version contains a lot of herbs with just a bit of bulgur wheat, lots of lemon and oil, some onion, and possibly some tomato.

For a truly authentic Middle Eastern tabouli, you only need about 14 cups of bulgur wheat, soaked or steamed until tender (a tip, if you have the time: soak the bulgur in lemon and olive oil along with chopped tomato, if using, for several hours rather than steaming or boiling; it softens the bulgur while allowing it to absorb more flavor).

Add 2 cups herbs (chopped by hand! no processing!) to that amount of bulgur, and drizzle with equal parts lemon juice and quality olive oil (1/3-1/2 cup of each). 1 cup parsley, 12 cup mint, and 12 cup cilantro are my favorites. Add a small chopped onion or sliced scallions (about 12 cup) and a chopped tomato if desired. There is no better tabouli than one made with fresh herbs from the garden.

Herbal teas or tisanes are another great way to put your herbs to use. I can tell you from personal experience that fresh mint tea with lots of sugar is just as good as any other afternoon pick-me-up. Simply pour lightly boiling water over a handful of fresh leaves, add sugar to taste, and, if you're feeling brave, sieve out the leaves after a few minutes of steeping.

To increase the flavor and caffeine content, add some green tea leaves or bags. Lemon verbena, a rarer herb that is quite strong when raw but fragrant and tasty when used for tea, is another excellent tea herb.

Finally, you can use your herbal bounty to make flavored syrups, which is a great way to save your herbs for later use. Make a sugar syrup by lightly boiling equal parts sugar and water (a little more water if using coarser raw sugar), then steep a handful of fresh herbs in it until cool to room temperature.

This will keep for several months if strained and refrigerated in a sterilized jar. Lemon verbena, lavender, mint, and basil are all lovely in this dish. You can make a variation on this method by steeping citrus peels alongside your herbs (lime loves mint, while basil enjoys lemon).

Add half a vanilla bean to any of these if you're feeling fancy for its exceptional flavor depth. These syrups can be used to flavor tea and cocktails, to drizzle over dessert, or to make sorbet.

Herbs, of course, are the finishing touch to many a dish, adding a distinct freshness of flavor to nearly anything, and you'll find countless uses for the ones in your garden. More ways to highlight your herbs include roast chicken stuffed with tarragon rolled omelet with chives, and bread stuffing laced with oregano and sage.

VEGETABLES

Lettuces

The first thing that comes to mind when thinking about lettuce is obviously a salad. A simple green salad with freshly picked lettuce is a true spring and early fall highlight. One word of caution when using homegrown lettuce: wash thoroughly! Your lettuce will undoubtedly contain dirt (and possibly a critter or two), and while this dirt may not be harmful to your health in an organic garden, it is unpleasantly gritty and not very tasty. Fill a clean sink halfway with cold water and add your lettuce; swish around for a minute, then let everything settle (the loose dirt will sink to the bottom of the sink).

Scoop the lettuce out with your hands, being careful not to disturb the dirt at the bottom, and drain on clean dish towels. I'd recommend harvesting twice or three times after a rain. Then, rinse the lettuce again to ensure that all grit has been removed, and spin it in a salad spinner. You can store lettuce in the fridge for an afternoon or overnight, wrapped in a clean flour sack towel; spread the lettuce over the entire towel, leaving some border, then carefully roll up. The towel absorbs excess moisture while also acting as a barrier against other fridge odors.

To dress your lettuce, all you need is a little acid, some oil, and a pinch of salt. Two vinaigrettes tips I've picked up on my travels: To begin, make a vinaigrette in your large salad bowl. Rub a garlic clove into the bowl, then add some Dijon mustard and one part acid (lemon, white or red wine vinegar, sherry, or balsamic vinegar) to two parts oil (extra virgin olive oil or walnut oil). Second, many older recipes call for one part acid to three parts oil; this feels heavy to modern cooks, especially on light and fresh lettuce. For best results, keep the ratio at 1:2.

Another important dressing to have in your arsenal is homemade ranch: trust me, you will never buy the bottled stuff again (and, in my opinion, using chemically laden bottled dressing is nearly criminal) on organic, fresh lettuce). In a clean jar, combine equal parts mayonnaise and buttermilk (say, 12 cup each), a couple of tablespoons each of freshly minced parsley and chives, and about half a teaspoon each of garlic salt and onion salt.

Shake vigorously to combine. If the mayonnaise is too thin, add more buttermilk; if the buttermilk is too thick, add more seasoning. Combine with blue cheese for a cobb salad or buffalo wing dip, or puree with tarragon and avocado for a green goddess-style dressing. This will keep in the fridge for a couple of weeks, though I doubt it will.

Greens

Greens are one of my favorite early spring and late fall harvests because they can be light and crunchy, rich and velvety, star and side, depending on how you prepare them. As with lettuce, the first step in making good food from garden greens is to thoroughly wash them! See the lettuce section above for some simple instructions on how to keep your greens clean.

I believe that erring on the side of excess washing with greens, especially when eating raw, is preferable to erring on the side of deficit. Little worms enjoy living in the greens; if you see their tell-tale holes in any leaves, thoroughly inspect them.

A classic spinach salad with warm bacon dressing is one of the first things I make in the spring. This method also works well with arugula or a combination of spinach and arugula. Prepare a large bowl of cleaned spinach and 4 or 5 thinly sliced mushrooms. In a skillet, cook 4 or 5 chopped bacon slices.

When the bacon is crisp and the fat has rendered, whisk in 2 tablespoons cider vinegar and 2 teaspoons brown sugar. If necessary, adjust the seasoning (additional vinegar and/or sugar, salt). Toss the salad with the warm dressing. 2 or 3 sliced hard-boiled eggs on top. This is a complete meal for two or a filling appetizer for four.

One of my favorite things to do with a fall harvest of greens (aside from traditional stewed collard greens: a Thanksgiving must) is to make a large pot of Mediterranean style chard or kale. Fill a large skillet (with a matching lid) halfway with cleaned chard as well as kale (you can mix them, but I find that using one or the other makes for a purer flavor).

Don't bother spinning the leaves dry because the water clinging to them aids in cooking. Add a third of a cup of cilantro, a small bunch of chopped scallions, a couple of minced garlic cloves, 14 cups or more of good olive oil, and a heaping tablespoon of smoked paprika to that. Allow that to wilt over medium heat, stirring carefully (because your pot should be literally overflowing with stuff), until the lid fits on top. Cover and cook for 20-30 minutes for chard and 30-40 minutes for kale on low heat. By adding a can of drained chickpeas, you can make this into a vegetarian main dish.

There's also the Southern staple of braised collard greens. Though there are numerous methods for doing so, I came across one that I think is even better than the traditional. Prepare your greens for stewing by stacking them, rolling them into a cigar shape, and slicing; this is a quick way to prep when you have a lot of greens. Heat some olive oil in a large pot and sauté the chopped onion and garlic (measurements depend on how many greens you're using and your personal taste).

Soften that a little, then add a handful of collard greens at a time, stirring as each batch wilts slightly, until all greens are incorporated and barely wilted. Add a smoked turkey wing (or smoked duck wing if you have access to it) and a cup or so of water.

Cook for a couple of hours, then remove the wing and shred the meat before returning it to the pot. If you like it spicy, add a few splashes of vinegar and some red pepper flakes. When I had ducks from hunting trips, I used to do this. I'd save the duck wings and skin to add to collard greens after smoking it. Rich and flavorful while remaining lighter than traditional salt pork seasoning.

All greens work well in salads, though heartier greens like mature Swiss chard, kale, and collards require a different approach. Thinly slice or finely chop these heartier greens and season with coarse salt and lemon juice; set aside for about an hour. The greens will soften slightly but retain their crunch. Toss with additional juice, oil, and salt to taste, and serve as is. Alternatively, add dried fruits like cranberries and toasted nuts.

Sugar Snap Peas

These little pods are sweet and neat, as the name suggests, and ready to eat right away. As a reward for my weeding efforts, I always have a few right off the vine. Certain varieties may require "stringing" by pinching the top off and pulling the fibrous string down the back of the pod, but this is only necessary if the fibrous string bothers you.

When sugar snap peas are in season, I throw them into salads or add them to a quick sauté whenever I have a few on hand. They go especially well with radishes, and a salad of thinly sliced peas and radishes requires only lemon and oil to dress.

My favorite early spring dish with snaps is a sautéed pea medley; if you've grown garlic, pick up an early head or two; this immature garlic, known at the market as green garlic, makes a wonderfully fragrant accompaniment.

Cook your sliced green garlic or spring onions in olive oil until softened, then add about a cup each of thinly sliced sugar snap peas and regular green peas (shelled or frozen).
Cook until the peas are tender but still crunchy. If you have pea tendrils, fava beans, and/or green almonds at your market, add them to the mix; the more the merrier. Top with minced herbs of your choice, such as mint, parsley, and/or tarragon.
I also enjoy them with steak salads, such as Thai beef salad: slice thinly leftover grilled steak and toss with crisp lettuce and sliced sugar snap peas. Make a dressing with equal parts lime and soy sauce (or, even better, half soy sauce and half fish sauce), and toss in some minced garlic and hot green chiles—the spicier, the better in my house. Pour over vegetables and steak after whisking in a dash of sugar. The snaps' green vegetal flavor shines through in this salty, funky, spicy dressing.

They are also delicious when sautéed or quickly roasted in a hot oven. Coat in oil and sauté over high heat or blast-roast in a very hot oven. Toss with a dash of toasted sesame oil and salt when lightly blistered, then sprinkle with sesame seeds.

Radishes

The radish is another lovely spring vegetable that adds crunch and a hint of spice to a variety of salads. They, like sugar snap peas, can be eaten raw with little to no preparation (just, of course, some cleaning). As previously stated, they pair well with sugar snap peas and can be used interchangeably in a variety of recipes.

My go-to radishes recipe is a crunchy relish that goes so well with spring lamb or pork that I make it several times throughout the spring and fall. A food processor is ideal for this, but chopping by hand can also work, albeit more slowly. In a food processor, combine 10 trimmed radishes with 14 cup of mint, parsley, or a combination of the two.

14 cup nuts, a few tablespoons lemon juice and olive oil, and pulse until coarsely chopped (adjust texture depending on how you're serving it: coarse for a salad-like presentation, finer for a relish). I use local pecans for this and occasionally add a seeded jalapeno and a minced garlic clove or two for a stronger flavor. Not only does it go well with grilled lamb or pork chops, but it's also delicious spooned into cooled, cooked rice with a dash of mayonnaise to combine (add some drained tuna for a non-vegetarian lunch).

Another unusual use for radishes, particularly the French breakfast radish, is to simply wash and trim radishes that have been chilled. Serve whole or halved with a pot of the best butter you can find or make at home and a saucer of coarse sea salt. Dip radishes in butter and then in salt. A divine lunch with some fresh baguette and charcuterie.

Trim and halve radishes (quarter if large), then soak in equal parts red wine vinegar and soy sauce for about an hour, turning a couple of times, for an Asian twist on the radish side dish. A salty, sour, crunchy accompaniment to a stir-fry or curry.

Cruciferous Veggies

Cabbages, broccoli, cauliflower, and Brussel sprouts are among the last vegetables to mature in the spring or fall seasons, and they are sweeter and heartier when grown at home. Almost every cook has a recipe or two for these common vegetables in their back pocket; hopefully, these few methods will give you some new ideas for how to use them.

Fresh, sweet cabbage from the garden begs for coleslaw, and most ambitious home cooks already have a recipe they use. I thinly slice the cabbage and salt it first, then drain it in a colander for an hour or two to ensure that the final slaw isn't watered down. Some people add carrots or purple cabbage to their slaw, which is fine (and pretty), but when I have fresh garden cabbage, I prefer to leave it alone.

I only use a small amount of mayonnaise, cider vinegar, and sugar; I prefer the slaw to taste like cabbage rather than mayonnaise and to be tart-sweet rather than sweet-tart. To deepen the flavor, toss in some chopped toasted pecans and/or fresh herbs.

Raw cabbage is also delicious on tacos, far superior to delicate lettuce, which is overpowered by the spicier, meatier flavor of most tacos. Before topping your taco or tostada, toss with lime and salt.

Cabbage can also be cooked (though some people dislike the sulfurous odor of cooked cabbage), and I love Southern-style smothered cabbage. Simply chop an onion and a small head of cabbage and place them in a large skillet with more butter than you think you need (a good half stick). Season with salt and pepper, cover, and cook on low for 45 minutes or more. Remove the lid, increase the heat, and allow it to brown slightly.

Broccoli, cauliflower, and Brussels sprouts all roast beautifully, creating a caramelized and even crunchy exterior while keeping the vegetable juicy and tender. I don't recommend cooking them as a medley because they each take different amounts of time to roast; also, don't crowd the pan when roasting for best results. If you have a sheet pan lined with aluminum foil, use it.

Toss in broccoli or cauliflower heads, or cut Brussel sprouts in half, sufficient quality olive oil to coat and roast at 425°F for 30-45 minutes, or until browned. Brussel sprouts with a splash of fish sauce and some Asian chile powder (shichimi togarashi, for example) sprinkled with toasted rice Krispies; broccoli with pine nuts and pecorino cheese; cauliflower with capers and walnuts; I know it sounds strange, but it is truly delicious and was inspired by David Chang of Momofuku.

I also enjoy making a broccoli and cauliflower casserole. Blanch equal parts broccoli and cauliflower for a few minutes in boiling salted water (do not overcook or your casserole will be mushy); drain well. With butter, flour, and milk, make a basic béchamel sauce. To make about a cup of béchamel, combine equal parts butter and flour (2 tablespoons) and cook over medium heat until the flour begins to color slightly, then slowly whisk in a cup of milk, stirring constantly to prevent lumps. Toss the vegetables with the béchamel, place in a greased baking dish (thinly spread out if you like the crunchy bits), and top with grated Gruyere cheese and panko bread crumbs. Other cheeses can be used, but the Gruyere enhances the flavor of the broccoli-cauliflower mixture.

Another great way to use broccoli and/or cauliflower is in soup: soup freezes well and is a great way to ensure that excess produce does not go to waste. A head of broccoli or cauliflower, a small onion, and some good quality vegetable or chicken stock are all you need. You can either leave it chunky or puree it (use an immersion blender for a quick coarse puree or whirl in a processor or blender).

You can add whatever else you want: potatoes or rice for starchy bulk; milk or cream for a silky-smooth puree; diced tomatoes and/or a handful of fresh corn kernels for acidity and sweetness; or, as my mother couldn't resist, a hefty serving of cheese. I'll forgive her for using Velveeta (I still love her version, despite my better instincts), but a good melting cheddar elevates the idea slightly.

Green Pole Beans
Sitting on a cool back porch and snapping beans is a well-known summer pastime. It's a chance to reflect on the recent spring while not worrying too much about the upcoming summer heat and potential drought.

I like to cook green beans in two ways: blanched and stewed. Blanching allows for an infinite number of variations, as you can toss quickly blanched beans with any number of vinaigrettes and add-ins. Simply blanch the beans in boiling salted water for 2 minutes for crisp and up to 5 minutes for near-tender.

Plunge into a bowl of ice water right away to stop the cooking and preserve the color. These can be refrigerated for a day or two before using, or frozen for later use (more on that in the next chapter). For an excellent side salad, dress with a red wine vinaigrette and toss in a bunch of slivered basil and some minced garlic. Toss with a walnut-oil vinaigrette and a handful of toasted walnuts, if desired.

Green bean and potato stew is a Southern cooking classic, and summer wouldn't be complete without a couple of pots of it. Combine a 12-ounce package of bacon, a pound of snapped green beans, and a pound of new potatoes, halved if large. Pour in a cup of water, season with salt and pepper, and leave to simmer for about an hour. Cooking is dead simple and requires only the most precious of commodities: absolutely fresh vegetables.

Okra
In the height of summer, the nearly invincible okra will sprout and proliferate in what appears to be minutes. Of course, almost everyone knows that fried okra is the way to go, but there are a few variations on that theme, as well as some lovely stewed okra preparations. One of okra's not-so-secret characteristics, sliminess, can be a boon or a bane depending on

what you're cooking. That gelatinous character can be an excellent thickener (think gumbo), but it can be off-putting in quick, stand-alone preparations. The top of the pod should be left alone.

Traditional fried okra involves cutting okra into rounds, tossing with cornmeal or a cornmeal-flour mixture, and pan-frying in vegetable oil. Of course, this is excellent, but for virtually slime-free results, cut pods in half, leaving the top trimmed but intact.

Dredge halved okra in flour and pan fry over high heat for Asian fried okra. You want the okra to be almost burnt. Toss with minced garlic and hot chiles, fresh basil and/or cilantro, and fish sauce or salt to taste. Okra can be served as a hors d'oeuvres when prepared in this manner.

If you ever make gumbo, okra is an essential ingredient (some people use file powder, but they wouldn't if they had Cajun relatives). However, stewed okra and tomatoes are another delicious way to use up some of your bumper crop. Put whole okra pods in a pot—smaller is better for this dish—and add about half as many chopped tomatoes (by volume); pour in a glug of olive oil and simmer for 30-40 minutes, or until tomatoes have dissolved and created a kind of okra sauce. The long cooking time, combined with the preparation of the entire pod, eliminates the typical mucilaginous texture. For extra flavor, toss in some fresh herbs and a squeeze of lemon.

Tomatoes

Garden ripe tomatoes have a plethora of uses, and even when unripe (fried green tomatoes, anyone?), tomatoes have their uses. It's easy to write an entire book on the use of tomatoes, but I'll limit myself to a few quick and simple preparations, as well as a couple of more involved but less common ideas. See the following chapter for methods of preserving tomatoes, such as sauce preparations.

After a long winter and spring deprived of the joys of a perfectly ripe, just off-the-vine tomato, the simplest and most anticipated way to eat tomatoes is to slice and serve. Friends request sliced tomatoes on a platter drizzled with the best olive oil I can afford, a splash of sherry vinegar (most people use balsamic vinegar; that's fine, too), slivered basil, and a sprinkle of blue cheese.

Intersperse sliced mozzarella (or, better yet, burrata) with tomato slices and sprinkle with basil; scatter capers (fried until crisp, if you're feeling adventurous) and olives over your platter of tomatoes; make a cheese cracker dough (equal parts flour, butter, and cheese), bake in a pie pan, and layer drained sliced tomatoes on top. Tomatoes pair well with almost any salty, savory, umami-laden ingredient you can find in your pantry or fridge.

Of course, cherry tomatoes come first, and they can be added to any salad or marinated in oil and vinegar (with or without garlic and herbs) and served as a side dish on their own. If you have too many to eat by themselves, roasted cherry tomatoes are delicious with grilled meats, especially fish: in a baking dish large enough to hold a single layer, toss in your cherry tomatoes and enough good olive oil to coat; there's no need to halve them, but I do recommend poking a tiny hole in each to prevent bursting and splattering. Sprinkle with sherry vinegar, tuck in some whole peeled garlic cloves, and garnish with oregano sprigs. Roast at 350°F for 30-40 minutes, or until tomatoes are soft and garlic is soft. Mash

Depending on how you serve it, you can mix everything together or leave it chunky. It's also delicious smeared on toasted bread. Of course, fresh summer tomatoes aren't complete without a salsa or two: Mexican with jalapenos, garlic, cilantro, and lime; Italian with olive oil, balsamic vinegar, garlic, and basil; Middle Eastern with olive oil, a lot of lemon juice, and tons of fresh parsley.

Gazpacho is a world-famous tomato preparation, with many variations ranging from the thin Andalusian-style cold soup to the thicker salmorejo style from Cordoba. There are also numerous variations with origins in the American Southwest. Given that I have an abundance of vine-ripened heirloom tomatoes, I am a purist when it comes to gazpacho. Tomatoes, excellent olive oil, and aged sherry vinegar are pureed and strained in their purest form; poured around a cold seafood salad and some sliced avocado, this is truly earth-shatteringly good, but entirely dependent on ingredients. Most Andalusian-style gazpacho recipes include water-soaked bread as a thickener, as well as cucumber and bell pepper.

Salmorejo is simply a thicker version with a higher bread-to-tomato ratio that is typically topped with crunchy croutons, chopped hard-boiled egg, and crisped Serrano ham.

A Moroccan-inspired cold tomato soup with spicier elements that is similar to gazpacho. Using a tablespoon of olive oil, gently cook a few minced garlic cloves, smoked paprika, and ground cumin until the garlic softens and the mixture is fragrant.

Grate a couple of pounds of tomatoes (or use a food mill if you have one), then add the oil-spice mixture, chopped cilantro, and a couple of stalks of diced celery. Add some lemon juice to brighten it up, salt to taste, and a splash of water to thin it out if necessary. Serve chilled.

With the addition of some acid and oil, as well as some garlic and herbs, grated tomatoes make an excellent marinade. When marinated, tomatoes help tenderize the meat. I particularly enjoy doing this with chicken, which I grill kebab-style.

During the peak of the season, I mostly indulge in raw tomato preparations, but there are a few exceptions. If I'm grilling, I always make stuffed tomatoes: place halved and seeded tomatoes in a baking pan that can be grilled, drizzle with olive oil, and stuff with a mixture of equal parts bread crumbs and grated parmesan, streaked through with chopped herbs (basil and oregano good, but tarragon also works for a different flavor). Grill until the tomatoes wilt and the cheese begins to brown. Of course, this can also be done in an oven.

Cucumbers

Cucumbers, like tomatoes, are a summertime delight that can be prepared simply and easily for an excellent fresh crunch to any meal. Slice and serve is fantastic, with only a splash of vinegar and salt required to make a side dish for almost any meal.

Quick pickles are also handy to have on hand as a side dish, in a sandwich, or as a relish. For most recipes, I seed my cucumbers because the seeds can be difficult to digest. Peel and seed a couple of cucumbers (if it's early season and the cucumbers are young and tender, leave the peel on); toss in a bowl with enough vinegar to coat, and season with equal parts salt and sugar. Place in a baggie and tightly seal, sucking out all the air. These can be eaten within a few hours or up to a couple of days of being prepared, and they obviously respond well to other seasonings, if desired.

Cucumber salsa is also a refreshing alternative to traditional tomato-based salsas. One of my favorites goes well with jerk chicken or pork and goes well with spicy grilled meats. 1 part cucumber, 1/2 part mango, and enough oil to coat Season with salt and toss with fresh herbs (thyme is particularly tasty here), minced scallions or onion, and seeded chile peppers.

Melons

Melons, like the other summer fruits mentioned above, are quick and simple to prepare: peel and cut or halve, seed, and eat with a spoon. Classic preparations include cantaloupe-style melon cut into wedges and draped with prosciutto or serrano ham; pickled melon rind; and melon with cottage cheese, a nod to old America. Melon, like tomatoes and cucumbers, can be used to make savory salads and salsas.

Another popular preparation in Latin American cultures is the melon cooler, which is one of many agua frescas served in markets and restaurants. Fill a blender halfway with cubed melon, then add 14 to 12 cup sugar (depending on how sweet your melon is) and a couple of tablespoons lime juice. Puree until very smooth, then divide between two pitchers and add a cup of ice water to each. To taste, add more sugar and/or lime.

Other Peppers and Chile

Chiles and other peppers are typically relegated to supporting roles, but many well-known cuisines would be incomplete without these hearty new-world ingredients. Fresh chiles are essential in salsas and add a spicy kick to stir fries and curries.

Many recipes call for roasted peppers, which are then peeled and seeded before use: the roasting enhances the flavor of the chile and adds a subtle smokiness. There are several approaches to this. If you're only roasting a couple of chiles for a dish and have a gas stove, simply remove the ring and roast the chiles directly in the flame for a few seconds on each side until the skin blackens and the chiles smell fragrant. Alternatively, position an oven rack at the top of your oven and preheat it to 450 degrees.

Roast chiles on a baking sheet, turning once or twice until the skins are charred. Use a large sheet pan lined with foil if you're roasting a lot of chiles for a batch of stew or sauce or for freezing. In this case, you may want to halve and seed your chiles before roasting them in a single layer on a baking sheet. This eliminates the need to turn chiles and makes de-seeding easier. Place roasted peppers in a paper bag to steam for a few minutes after roasting to make peeling easier.

Peppers can also be stuffed, as in the recent trend of jalapeno poppers on menus, or in more refined dishes like chiles en nogada, a Mexican holiday specialty. When I have large Anaheim or poblanos in the garden, I like to stuff them with cheese or ground beef cooked with garlic and cumin (or a combination), then carefully coat in tempura batter and deep fry until the batter puffs and the cheese melts. I keep a quick tempura batter mix on hand: combine three cups cake flour, 34 cup cornstarch, and leaven with a couple of teaspoons baking soda; season with a teaspoon or two salt. Mix with seltzer water to make a batter when ready to use (usually, a ration of two parts batter to one part liquid). Serve with chiles If you have it, serve the rellenos with a smooth enchilada sauce or fresh salsa.

Squash and similar vegetables

Squash is another abundant crop, whether in the summer (yellow crookneck, zucchini) or in the fall (acorn, butternut). Squash is virtually trouble-free to grow and lends itself to a variety of simple recipes.

One of my favorites is zucchini-corn sauté; it makes an excellent vegetable side dish to serve alongside enchiladas or tacos. Slice a couple of zucchinis into half-moons, then sauté in a large skillet for a few minutes; add a cup or so of corn kernels, preferably fresh off the cob, and cook until both zucchini and corn begin to brown. Finish with a squeeze of lime juice and a sprinkle of cilantro.

Squash can also be hollowed out and stuffed before baking for an elegant summer side dish. Sauté the squash insides with garlic, onion, and herbs in a skillet, then add cooked rice or crispy breadcrumbs and return to the squash shells. Bake until the shells are tender, then top with more breadcrumbs and/or grated hard cheese. I occasionally add black olives to the mix for a salty kick.

Acorn squash is a lovely fall squash that works well for stuffing: simply cut in half and scoop out the stringy flesh and seeds, then stuff with a filling like a big pat of butter and cinnamon mixed with brown sugar, or crumbled Italian sausage spiked with maple syrup. The squash is left unpeeled, but the skins aren't edible; scoop out servings or serve half a squash as an entrée. Make a slice off the underside of the squash to keep it flat while baking.

Alliums (Garlic & Onions & Leeks)
Alliums are another group of supporting players that appear almost everywhere in cooking. Here are a few recipe ideas that highlight each of these typically supporting characters.

A famous French preparation of chicken with 40 cloves of garlic is a delicious way to make your house smell warm and inviting. Essentially, this is a garlicky roast chicken. I prefer to spatchcock a whole chicken (removing the backbone, then flipping the chicken and breaking the breastbone, flattening it—allows for more even cooking), but you can cut a whole chicken into pieces if you prefer.

In a roasting pan, drizzle a thin layer of olive oil and place your chicken or chicken pieces, skin side up. Sprinkle with peeled garlic cloves and sprigs of fresh chicken or tarragon, if desired. Cover with foil (or use an oven-safe pan with a lid) and bake for an hour at 350 degrees. Make sure you have plenty of crusty bread on hand to spread the soft garlic cloves on.

Caramelized onions are one of those kitchen staples that you should always have on hand: make more than you think you'll need and freeze the extra for later use. All you need is a nonstick pan, preferably with butter and/or oil, a large amount of onions of any color, and some patience.

Cook sliced onions in butter or oil (I use a combination) over low heat, stirring occasionally, until dark brown, up to an hour and a half. Serve alongside grilled meats, on top of burgers and sausages, or on homemade pizza. When I think of leeks and potatoes during the season, I think of vichyssoise, a cold pureed French soup. It's simple to make and filling while remaining light. In some butter, sauté equal parts leeks and potatoes (only use white and light green parts of leek and peel potatoes).

Cover with chicken stock and, if desired, garnish with a bay leaf and herb sprigs. Simmer until the leeks and potatoes are soft. Blend until smooth, then set aside to cool before adding a splash of cream or half and half. Chill before serving with sliced chives on top, 5 leeks, 5 potatoes, and 5 cups chicken stock make about 4 servings.

Potatoes

This hearty vegetable, common on the American table, lends itself to almost any preparation: baked, boiled, fried, roasted, scalloped, and pancaked, most home cooks have a handy collection of potato recipes on hand. I've already mentioned them as supporting players in dishes like green bean and potato stew and potato-leek soup (vichyssoise). Here are some more unusual recipes for the humble potato.

While we don't often think of potatoes as a suitable vegetable for stir-frying, many places in China have adopted the potato; in the south, you'll find Sichuan-style stir-fried potatoes. These potatoes are very different from your typical roasted or baked potatoes because they are cooked quickly and left slightly crunchy. Peel and cut a pound and a half of potatoes into matchstick-sized slivers.

Soak them in cold salted water for a few minutes to remove the starch. Drain thoroughly. Cook a half-dozen small dried red chiles (leave them whole) and a teaspoon or two Sichuan peppercorns for a couple of minutes in a wok or heavy skillet until fragrant. Stir in the matchstick potatoes and season with salt for another 5 minutes. Serve with toasted sesame oil drizzled on top.

Another interesting and unique way to prepare potatoes comes from Spain. Patatas bravas (brave potatoes) are a staple of a tapas-style spread, best served with small red or white potatoes that are creamy rather than fluffy. Boil potatoes whole until tender, then smash and lightly coat with oil. Spread potatoes in a single layer on a baking sheet and roast for 35-45 minutes, or until very brown and crunchy. Meanwhile, prepare the brava sauce by sautéing a small chopped onion, some garlic, and a can of tomatoes (or your own, roasted and peeled) until the onion is very tender. Allow cooling slightly before pureeing in a blender or processor with a couple teaspoons smoked paprika.

Serve with homemade mayonnaise over potatoes or on the side for dipping. (Do you have no idea how to make homemade mayonnaise? It's simple and delicious: whisk together one egg, one egg yolk, some lemon juice, a splash of Dijon mustard, and some parsley.

Blend or process the salt until it is just combined. Drizzle in very fresh olive oil, about 34 cups at a time, until mixture is emulsified.)

Chapter Six

PRESERVING TECHNIQUES: GARDENING WITH ZERO WASTE

After months of planning, planting, and growing, the last thing a gardener wants to do is waste any of his or her harvests. If like me, you have a small plot and are only planting a few things, you may be able to use everything you grow as you pick it. However, if you, like me, find that you are better than expected at gardening—an unexpected pleasure—you may have to devise ways to avoid wasting your crops.

Furthermore, many people, including myself, simply want to save something from spring and summer to last them through the long winter months. Nothing lifts the spirits like cracking open a can of cucumber pickles or rescuing a freezer bag full of homemade tomato sauce in February (unless you live in southern Arizona, of course). There are numerous methods for successfully maintaining a "zero waste" garden, ranging from complex to simple.

Not to be forgotten: feeding your compost pile is one of the simplest ways to ensure that no fruit, vegetable, stem, or vine goes to waste in your garden. Any inedible or undesirable skin, core, or bird-picked fruit should be discarded (or, alas, the occasional neglected scrap at the bottom of the vegetable bin).

When one season ends and you're clearing away the last roots from your spring plants or vines from your summer plants, grind them up as best you can and toss them in with the pile. Your garden is fed each year by the garden of the previous year, a true cycle of life (to paraphrase a famous film). Canning, freezing, dehydrating (drying), fermenting, and smoking are some other creative ways to preserve your crops throughout the year. See below for more information on each method, as well as some recipe ideas.

Canning

Canning is a nearly foolproof way to preserve your harvest for months, if not years, to come. However, it is a lost art among most home cooks. Supermarkets have made it far too easy to get whatever product you want, whenever you want it. While there is nothing inherently wrong with this, growing and preserving your own food is both economically and environmentally sound. Canning is a time-honored method for accomplishing this.

A water bath canner and/or a pressure canner, canning jars (mason jars, such as Ball and Kerr) with lids, and a jar lifter are all required for canning. If you are serious about canning, you should know that there are two types of canning that are considered safe for long-term preservation: water bath canning for high acid products and pressure canning for low acid products. As a result, if you want to can fresh vegetables from your garden, you'll need to invest in a pressure canner.

If you want to can sauces, pickles, or jellies made from garden produce, a water bath canner should suffice. The Ball Kerr company has an excellent website with information on how to obtain canning equipment and how to can safely; click here for more information.

I've done some canning in the past, but I don't produce enough to justify the time investment. I strongly advise you to learn if you acquire a large plot of land on which to grow numerous plants of each variety. For those of us who live in suburbs or cities and have small raised beds, freezing is a more practical way to keep fruits and vegetables over the winter.

Freezing

If like me, you don't have the time, space, or equipment to do much canning, and you don't have a large enough garden to need to save a harvest for more than a few months, freezing is your best option. Aside from your produce, the only tools you'll need are sturdy storage bags—quart size is best for ease of storage and portion size—and a black sharpie.

While many fruits and vegetables freeze well, others do not. It is not recommended to freeze lettuce or radishes. A general rule of thumb is that if the product can be blanched without drastically altering its properties, it can be frozen. Green beans, for example, are excellent for freezing: blanch them in boiling salted water for a few minutes; shock them quickly in ice water to stop cooking and preserve color; then dry and place on a sheet pan or cookie tray in a single layer; place in freezer until frozen; then pack into a freezer bag labeling the contents and—most importantly—the date it was frozen.

Most vegetables will keep for about six months if properly stored, but after that, they lose flavor and can become frostbitten. Sugar snap peas, broccoli, cauliflower, Brussel sprouts, and some low moisture squashes can all be blanched and frozen using the method described above.

Greens of all types respond well to this, though the method differs slightly: blanch hearty greens like kale and collards for about five minutes, while softer greens like spinach and chard only take a minute or two. Drain in a colander and rinse with cold water once blanched. To speed up the cooling process, I sometimes throw a handful of ice cubes on top, but you have to pick bits of green off the cubes. I don't like using an ice bath on greens because I believe it waterlogs them too much. When the greens are cool enough to handle, squeeze out as much liquid as possible and coarsely chop before placing in a labeled freezer bag. Other vegetables, such as okra and cucumbers, benefit more from this method. Some kind of pickling (see the fermenting section below for details on that).

Potatoes can also be frozen in this manner for making french fries. Blanch until lightly cooked but not colored in hot oil; drain well and pat dry before freezing in a single layer on a baking sheet. Put them in your prepared freezer bags and cook them in hot oil (about 325 to 350 degrees) until browned and crunchy when ready to eat. There is no need to defrost.

Roasting is another method for preparing certain crops for freezing. Roasted peppers are excellent candidates for freezing (see Chapter 5 for more information on roasting peppers), and I like to make a mixed bag of roasted peppers—jalapenos, poblanos, and anaheims—to pull out during the winter to make green chile stew. So, if you don't have enough of one type to freeze, create a "house blend."

Tomatoes are also excellent for roasting, and each season, I stock up on several freezer bags of both plain roasted tomatoes and tomato sauces. To make the best-roasted tomatoes, core each tomato and score an X in the bottom end; place tomatoes in a single layer, core side down, on a foil-lined baking sheet. Roast for about ten minutes at 450 degrees (timing depends on the size and ripeness of the tomatoes; use your best judgment, as there really isn't a way to fail at this), until the tomatoes emit juice and the X begins to curl the skin back. The skin should easily peel off, but the tomatoes should not fall to mush (though, if they do, no matter: still usable). When the tomatoes are cool enough to handle, peel and, if desired, squeeze them to release most of the juice and seeds before placing them in labeled freezer bags.

This method is the most similar to what you'd find in a supermarket can of whole tomatoes (though large heirloom varieties typically have a higher moisture content). Another tip: do not discard the roasted tomato juice! Simply strain through a fine sieve to remove the seeds and skin; season with salt and lemon or lime juice to taste; and drink for breakfast or in a delicious Bloody Mary.

I also enjoy making sauces with the roasted tomatoes. In a good harvest year, I save three or four bags of plain roasted tomatoes and two or three bags of each of three ready-made sauces.

The first is a simple Italian red sauce, which is delicious on spaghetti with just a sprinkle of cheese or in baked pasta dishes or Italian-inspired roasts. Almost every ingredient in this comes directly from my lovely little organic garden most of the time. In a quality olive oil, sauté a coarsely chopped yellow or white onion and garlic (be generous: it is Italian cooking, after all). When the onion and garlic are softened, add 8 to 10 roasted, skinned, and seeded tomatoes, crushing them lightly with your hands as you go. Add a half-dozen large basil leaves, season with salt, and simmer for 20-30 minutes. You want the flavors to combine and all of the ingredients to be soft, but with some liquid remaining.

Allow everything to cool before whirling in the food processor with another half dozen basil leaves. You could also use oregano or a combination of basil and oregano here. I use basil in sauces instead of drying it because basil does not dry well. Fill your freezer bag with sauce and label it: the above recipe should fit in a standard quart-sized bag.

The second is an even simpler chipotle sauce inspired by Mexico for enchiladas or fideo dishes. 8 to 10 roasted, skinned, seeded tomatoes pureed with 2 or 3 canned or homemade chipotle peppers (see below) and salt if you want a more complex sauce, sauté some onion and garlic until soft before adding to the above. Place in freezer bags that have been prepared.

The third is a Mediterranean-style tomato sauce that goes well with grilled meats and kebabs as well as meatballs or chickpeas. In a small pan, sauté some chopped garlic in a generous amount of good olive oil until softened, then add a couple of teaspoons each of smoked paprika and cumin, as well as a teaspoon of Aleppo pepper (a marvelous coarse flaked dried pepper with hints of tartness and mild heat: well worth seeking out). Allow the mixture to cook for a minute or two, until the spices "bloom," then pour over your roasted, skinned, and peeled potatoes.

8 to 10 seeded tomatoes in a food processor or blender Add the salt and pulse until combined. If it needs more acid, squeeze in some lemon juice, or add a pinch of sugar. Place in freezer bags that have been prepared. Again, if you have a pressure canner, all of these recipe suggestions can be canned.

Dehydrating (Drying)

Even if you don't have a specialized home dehydrator, there are a few simple ways to save some of your harvest for later use. A dehydrator is useful if you want to make things like fruit leathers or vegetable chips, but you can stock your pantry all winter with just a little patience and care.

Herbs are the most obvious candidates for dehydrating, and drying your own herbs produces a far superior product than the vast majority of commercially processed herbs on the market. Certain herbs dry more easily than others; basil and chives both lose too much flavor in the process (and basil rots before it completely dries), so I don't bother with them.

However, tarragon, oregano, and mint dry particularly well, and the process couldn't be easier: at the end of the growing season, pull up your plant if you don't want to overwinter it, or cut it all back if you do (keep the mint, of course), and wash thoroughly. Because dust is nearly impossible to remove from dried leaves, don't skimp on the washing.

For a couple of weeks, place the plants on a large sheet tray and place it on top of your refrigerator (or another cool, dry place). Once dry, remove the leaves from the plants and store them in airtight containers away from direct sunlight. These should remain fresh and fragrant until the following year's harvest.

Many people also use a microwave to speed up the drying process. It's much faster—just microwave in short ten-second bursts until the herbs are dry—but I'm always afraid I'll "cook" the herbs instead of preserving their fresh flavor. Drying herbs and other small crops in the oven over the lowest heat setting is another option; depending on what you're drying, this can take anywhere from two to ten hours.

Again, this type of heat-based drying will alter the properties slightly. However, oven drying is ideal for making "sun-dried" tomatoes from smaller paste tomatoes like Roma. Peppers are another excellent candidate for drying. Once you've made your own pure chile powders, you'll inevitably want to sell them.

Most commercial brands leave me cold. I make a ristra (wreath) of cayenne peppers throughout the season, threading them onto a string as they ripen. To thread peppers, simply insert a needle threaded with a double layer of sturdy string tied off at the end through the pepper's stem, slide it down, and then insert the next one. Hang it on your kitchen windowsill or another bright spot where you'll remember it.

As I previously stated, simply add as peppers turn a bright red, and once the growing season is over and all are thoroughly dried, grind in a clean coffee or spice grinder until the consistency is to your liking. If you like, save some whole to add a punch to soups, stews, stocks, or stir-fries.

The ristra method described above works well for small, skinny peppers but not so well for thicker, juicier peppers like jalapenos and poblanos. Because of their size and moisture content, these peppers are more likely to rot before drying unless you have a dehydrator. Furthermore, these peppers are commonly used smoked, transforming into chipotles and anchos, respectively. Quick ideas are provided below.

Smoking

Smoking is another effective way to preserve certain crops if you have a backyard smoker. It is essentially a time-consuming method of drying foods while adding a layer of smoke flavor. If you don't have a backyard smoker or a wood-fired grill, a propane grill can be used, though it will use a lot of fuel. Remember your garden whenever you're getting ready to do some smoking: prepare a ristra of jalapenos and/or poblanos. This is usually done when the peppers are very ripe and have turned red. They are used fresh or roasted while still green. Make sure they're hanging close together so the string doesn't burn, and cut a long slit in each pepper to help the juices drain faster. (In fact, it's best if you harvest the peppers a week or so ahead of time and let them dry out a bit before smoking; this reduces the amount of time they'll spend in the pit.)

Remove them from the smoker once they have shriveled and hardened. Make sure they are completely dry or they will spoil (if they are still slightly moist, place them in prepared freezer bags; they will still be fine).

Dried chipotles can be used in the same way as commercially canned chipotles, but they must first be rehydrated in soaking liquid. They won't taste the same without the adobo sauce that comes with them in the can, but you can make your own and keep your dried chipotles in it in the fridge for a couple of months. Tomatoes, onions, garlic, cumin, oregano, and dried milder chiles or chile powder are common ingredients.

Other products that work well in the smoker include tomatoes, particularly smaller paste varieties like Roma, which can be halved and smoke-dried. Larger varieties of tomatoes will not necessarily keep longer in the pantry, but they can be stored and frozen like roasted tomatoes with a smoky kick: these make the most delicious tomato soup in the known universe.

Fermentation, Pickling, and Other Techniques
I've compiled a collection of ideas for preserving vegetables and fruits that I've used over the years. Almost everything I mention here will require refrigeration or freezing at some point, though almost everything here lends itself well to canning if you have the time and resources.

Fermented foods have made a comeback in recent years, with a growing consensus indicating that the active cultures, or probiotics, found in naturally fermented foods are remarkably beneficial to our overall health, particularly in maintaining a healthy digestive system. Pickles sold in supermarkets are typically heat-treated or pickled with vinegar rather than fermentation; both of these methods effectively kill any active microorganisms. If carefully monitored, naturally fermented or "pickled" vegetables made at home contain a plethora of good probiotics and taste superior to mass-produced items.

Kimchi, or fermented vegetables, are no longer an exotic food, thanks to the rapidly growing popularity of Korean food throughout the country. Most grocery stores sell jars of cabbage kimchi, but making it at home with your own organic produce is tastier, fresher, and healthier. While some of us are more familiar with sauerkraut, another traditional fermented cabbage dish, cabbage kimchi is spicier and livelier, as well as relatively easy to make.

To make cabbage kimchi at home, first, brine your cabbage by immersing it in a brine of 6 cups of water and 3 tablespoons of salt. Allow the cabbage to sit overnight after weighing it down with a plate topped with cans.

The next day, drain cabbage, reserving brine, and combine with half a dozen sliced scallions, half a dozen minced garlic cloves, a tablespoon or two of grated fresh ginger, two or three tablespoons of chile powder (gochugaru is the traditional Korean chile powder, but cayenne or other spicy chile powders can be substituted in a pinch), and a couple teaspoons of sugar.

Make sure the spices thoroughly coat the cabbage leaves before packing them into sterilized quart jars (I used to use old mayonnaise jars when they were glass; I'd avoid the new plastic ones) and pour in just enough reserved brine to cover. Put the remaining brine into sealable plastic baggies and push them into the mouth of the jar; this allows fermentation bubbles to escape (if you screw a lid on top, the jar may shatter) while preventing scum from forming on top.

Place in a cool, dark place for three to seven days (ideally no hotter than 70 degrees; I use the garage in the winter). Each day, it will become slightly fizzy and sourer. Remove baggies, pour brine back into jar, seal, and refrigerate when it's as sour as you like it (if doing this in hot weather, err on the side of sooner rather than later). This will keep for at least six months. This kimchi method also works well with radishes, cucumbers, and members of the allium family (I like a mix of leeks, onions, and garlic), and you can easily adapt this basic recipe to your preferences. To amp up the funk, some kimchi recipes call for the addition of dried shrimp or fish sauce.

Other types of pickling require vinegar, which, while not as high in probiotics, is still a delicious and healthy way to preserve your harvest. Again, unless you have canning equipment, these recipes must be kept refrigerated.

A simple pickling brine can be made by combining equal parts vinegar and water with enough salt to flavor and preserve the pickles. Pickling salt, which is simply table salt without the iodine, is used in many recipes because it dissolves faster in brines than kosher or sea salt. I never bother with it because it has no effect on me. I usually use kosher salt because it contains no additives; simply increase the amount called for to account for the coarser grains and ensure that it dissolves completely.

So, for about 2 pints of vegetables, 2 cups of cider vinegar, 2 cups of water, and 1 tablespoon plus a pinch more kosher salt make a great basic pickling liquid. Bring the brine to a boil, stirring to dissolve the salt, and then pour it over the vegetables in the sterilized jars. Add aromatics such as garlic cloves and dried peppers for variety and flavor; add as much sugar as salt for sweet and salty flavor.

Sour versions; experiment with different vinegars. Many vegetables, including okra and green beans, respond well to this: avoid sugar and add garlic and peppers. If you aren't canning these, make sure to blanch them first. Use the lighter rice wine vinegar and some sugar to make pickled garlic and cucumbers. Add peeled and sliced beet to some pickled radishes for a lovely blush color and natural sweetness. This method of making pickles can also be frozen for longer storage.

Other techniques include preserving in oil, vinegar, salt, and sugar. All of these elements promote longer storage and/or enhance the flavors of certain appropriate produce.

You can, for example, make flavored oils. Warm the oil, then add your aromatics of choice: herbs, fresh or dried; garlic cloves; chiles, fresh or dried; and/or dried tomatoes. Steep for a day or two before straining and storing in a cool, dark place for a few months. Citrus peels and whole spices can also be added to enhance the flavor.

This method also works for vinegars, though no heating is required and straining isn't always necessary because vinegar's acidity keeps the produce from spoiling. I love tarragon vinegar, and I believe that the delicate flavor of rice wine vinegar best preserves the tarragon flavor.

Refrigerated salted vegetables can last for a long time. Simply pack into crocks with salt layers and fish out bits for seasoning. Rinse the salt off and use sparingly because anything left in this state will become extremely salty. Consider preserved lemons or salt-packed capers as examples: salted radishes, for example, pack a lovely salty-spicy punch. This method can also be used with miso, a fermented soybean paste popular in Asian cooking. Of course, sugar is used in the preservation of fruits that lend themselves well to jams and jellies, and I enjoy making hot pepper jelly at the end of the season on occasion.

Finally, pepper water is a condiment-tonic that I keep in the fridge. 4 chopped hot peppers in a sterilized jar (serrano, jalapeno, Thai, cayenne, or a mix). To your peppers, add a couple of tablespoons of cider vinegar, a teaspoon of soy sauce, a teaspoon of fish sauce, a bay leaf, and a couple of crushed garlic cloves. Bring 10 ounces of water to a boil before pouring it over the ingredients in a jar. Allow it to cool slightly before refrigerating it, where it will keep indefinitely. Sprinkle it on plain rice; use it to add tart heat to soups, stews, curries, and the like; or mix it into plain tomato juice or a Bloody Mary. Or simply sip a sip or two after dinner.

Chapter Seven

KEEPING THE SEASONS: MAKING THE MOST OF YOUR GARDEN FOR ALL YEAR

While many of these tips and techniques have been briefly discussed in other chapters, this section provides more detailed information on how to care for your organic garden during each season. Of course, the goal is to maximize yield throughout the year while also maintaining soil health and sustainability.

Overwintering

There are three things you can do to ensure that your garden has a healthy winter season: Continue to grow appropriate crops; two, plant a cover crop that will reenergize your soil with nutrients while also providing warming ground cover; and three, mulch the garden well to prevent topsoil degradation. Of course, you can use a combination of all three.

As discussed in Chapter 3, overwintering crops include garlic, onion, and leeks. Certain root vegetable crops, such as potatoes, parsnips, and carrots, can also be overwintered. If you live in a region where winters aren't too cold for too long—that is, the ground doesn't freeze solid for an extended period—you can overwinter a variety of greens, including collards, kale, and heartier varieties of spinach and arugula.

Remember that if you leave crops in the ground for harvesting in the spring, you must protect your garden with mulch and clearly mark where plants are located to avoid accidentally digging them up when you turn your garden over for spring planting. Also, keep in mind that continuously planting can sometimes exhaust your soil; you can avoid this by feeding your garden rich, organic compost regularly or by giving it a winter break and planting an appropriate cover crop.

Cover crops are plants grown to improve soil health rather than crops grown for human consumption. Field peas, alfalfa, vetch, and some cereal grains are examples (oats, barley, rye, buckwheat). The best crops to grow depend on where you live, what your soil requires, and how long you plan to keep the cover crop.

Field peas and buckwheat are ideal for a short overwintering period. Cover crops not only return nutrients to the soil, but they also keep weeds at bay, attract beneficial insects, and act as organic mulch. If your garden seems to produce less than usual one growing season, or if you encounter diseases caused by poor soil health, resting it with a couple of months of cover crops will rejuvenate it. When you're ready to turn the garden and plant for the season,

In the spring, your cover crops make excellent compost pile fodder. If you don't have the time or desire to plant during the winter, do your garden a favor by mulching thoroughly. Mulch also helps to keep weeds at bay and keeps your soil warm and moist.

It also protects any crops that have gone dormant over the winter but will reappear in the spring. Be aware that different mulches will affect your soil in different ways, and, of course, look for organic mulches from reputable sources.

Many biodegradable mulches, such as lawn clippings, raked leaves, or straw, are readily available and have the added benefit of being easily tilled back into the soil. Just make certain that they are not chemically treated. Wood chip mulches are the most effective at providing winter warmth for your soil; cedar or eucalyptus mulch also serves as a natural insect repellant. Again, for specific advice about your area, consult your local garden shop, farmers' market, or cooperative extension. Finally, remember to tend to your compost in the winter, adding organic materials and ensuring it is well covered and continuing to decompose.

Spring Preparation

The first thing you should do before the start of the growing season is to have your soil tested. Determine whether your soil has the proper pH (6.5 is ideal) and whether it is deficient in certain nutrients (or, occasionally, has too much of some). You can do this at home with a soil testing kit, though the information provided is limited and lacks the benefit of an expert advising you on how to correct your soil, if necessary.

If your area has a cooperative extension service, the best place to get your soil tested is there. If you don't live near an extension service, there are resources available online. For links, see the USDA resources listed below. In the absence of that, speak with a local farmer from your market or a gardening expert in your area.

Next, thoroughly turn your garden, taking care not to disturb any overwintered crops. If you have a larger garden, this is where you might want to use a tiller. Turning soil breaks up any unwanted roots that may be present, as well as aerates and prepares the soil for planting. Add your compost and organic fertilizer at this time, and be sure to thoroughly till this material into your garden before planting.

If the soil in your area isn't suitable for gardening—for example, if it's mostly clay—you'll want to create your topsoil layer with organically sourced soil. Depending on the size of your plot, you can buy gardening soil at many large retail outlets (look for organic) and gardening shops.

If you have a lot of ground to cover, you can also look to local farmers and/or cooperative extension services to find out where you can buy soil in bulk. Unless something goes wrong, you should only need to do this in your first year of gardening because the compost you keep should provide you with plenty of healthy new soil to add each year.

This is the time of year when you should plan your garden space, organizing crops according to some basic rules of seasonality, succession planting, and companion planting, with an eye on the practical logistics of space, weed control, and ease of maintenance. Herb plants that will be snipped throughout the spring and summer should be easily accessible; for example, a long, squat raised bed plot should promote ease of harvesting with all crops.

Certainly, spring is the time of year when you will do the majority of your planting. Again, timing depends on your region or agricultural zone (see Chapter 1), but you should direct seed lettuces, greens, radishes, and cruciferous vegetables in early spring while transplanting seedlings like tomatoes, herbs, and chile peppers in mid-spring. See Chapter 3 for information on how and when to plant a variety of vegetables that are suitable for organic gardening.

Continuing Throughout the Summer
Summer brings its own set of challenges, depending on where you live. Summers will be hot and dry for the majority of us, though to what extent we have no control. Typically, this is also the time of year when weeds and pests

are at their most visible. It's also a great time of year for your garden to be at its most productive, so plan on regular harvesting and preserving. Recipes and preservation methods are covered in Chapters 5 and 6.

Most summer issues are combated or controlled by pre-existing preparations, such as companion planting to provide shade for plants susceptible to heat, drip irrigation to provide precise watering to the most important plants when it gets dry, and mulching with appropriate materials to control weeds and keep moisture in the soil.

Prepare to visit your garden every day—ideally, once in the morning and once in the evening—to keep up with weeds, pests, and diseases. More specific advice on dealing with these can be found in Chapter 4. Also, harvest on a daily basis to avoid losing a fruit or vegetable due to overgrowth or pest invasion, as well as to keep the plants healthy and productive.

Extending Into Autumn

The importance of succession planting cannot be overstated, and as discussed in Chapter 3, several crops that perform well in the spring can be replanted for an additional fall crop. The more actively you cultivate your garden, the healthier it will be, and while fall heralds the cold, nearly dormant season of winter, it can also be a beautiful time to garden. Pests are fewer, weeds are dying back, and diseases are dissipating.

Planting crops that will overwinter in the fall is ideal, such as garlic, onions, leeks, and various root vegetables or hearty greens. While some of these will not be harvested until the following year (garlic, onions, and some root vegetables), you can maximize your harvest by cultivating some fall spinach or other greens in certain areas to eat through Thanksgiving, then cutting the plants back before winter mulching; these will be among the first to poke their green heads up again in spring.

Consider cruciferous vegetables, some lettuces and greens, and autumn squashes as fall crops as well. When it comes to planting a fall garden, timing is everything: it is difficult to germinate seeds in the hot, dry summer, but your plants need time to mature before the first hard freeze of winter. Many plants will survive a frost, and some will even benefit from it in terms of flavor. If your summers are hot and your autumns are it is best to cultivate your seedlings inside for a month or two before transplanting to your garden outdoors.

Chapter Eigth

IMAGINING YOUR INFLUENCE: THE BIG PAYOFF

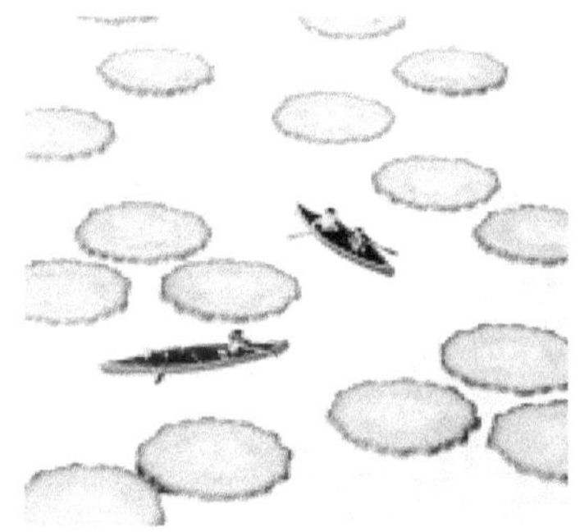

Now that you've accomplished your goal of becoming a successful backyard gardener, take a moment to consider the far-reaching impact of your efforts. You are not only providing healthy, nourishing food for yourself, your family, and your friends, but you are also reducing your carbon footprint and participating in a movement that promotes sustainability and accountability.

To say the least, the modern American relationship with food is torturous. From the inevitability of our Fast Food Nation to our passive acceptance of Dinner at the New Gene Café to agonizing deliberation over The Omnivore's Dilemma (to use compelling titles of recent books), the reasonably informed consumer may be justified in throwing up his or her hands in dismay.

The corporate takeover of our foodways is no longer limited to the economic dominance of the convenience industry—fast food, supermarket chains, big box stores—and its partners in industrial agriculture, but is increasingly being relegated to scientists and global genetic engineering behemoths.

Behind these contentious issues is a vexing issue: how to produce authentically nutritious and delicious food. Seasonal food, sustainable agriculture, and locally grown, preferably organic, produce have emerged as rallying cries for the new resistance.

 In an age of globalization—asparagus from South America in the dead of winter, even at a Whole Foods market—and in a country where public discourse continues to perplex even the most conscientious consumer, the question of how to feed our families well becomes an essential part of the campaign to restore an ethically compromised system of food production, distribution, and consumption.

There is no other way to put it: organically grown food is healthier. It nourishes both our bodies and the environment in ways that industrial agriculture cannot. Gardening organically allows you to grow tastier food with more nutrients in a shorter amount of time, a short distance from your back door.

Furthermore, as we all know, organic gardening improves our soil, water, and air by avoiding the use of petrochemicals and instead relying on the development of a natural micro biome that cycles and recycles its main ingredients in order to thrive.

First and foremost, your impact is felt—literally. Food grown with your own diligent labor is both more satisfying and more delicious. The majority of agricultural produce is bred (or modified) for heartiness and convenience rather than taste.

A bland supermarket tomato or mushy apple has been treated to ship well and look appealing, with little regard for taste quality or nutritional value. It goes without saying that harvesting your evening meal—even if only a small portion of it—from your own backyard or terrace is a tremendous sensual and psychological pleasure.

This clearly creates a sense of accountability: if you rely on your soil and environment for your own food, you begin to actively support those things, even if they are not on your own plot of land. This breaks a cycle in which corporate control of our foodways appears to be our only option. There are other options available to us.

Consider your garden as a source of inspiration. No matter how frustrating gardening can be at times, when the weather is too hot, too cold, too wet, or too dry, it is nothing short of miraculous to create life from the soil. By practicing organic gardening, you set a good example for your children, family, friends, and neighbors. Good habits spread, and I can tell you from personal experience that after a couple of seasons of gardening in my suburb, I had the pleasure of talking to neighbors from all over the area who would knock on my door for advice. I assisted a few neighbors in establishing their own gardens, and I'm sure they inspired others.

In what was once a rather drab neighborhood with clipped lawns, identical hedgerows, and meticulously pruned trees, became a veritable garden oasis—colorful, riotous, delectable, and healthy. A local farmers' market sprouted up as a result of this within a few years. Impacts can generate waves of inspiration.

Second, your involvement in the relatively simple and enormously satisfying act of organic gardening has an impact that extends beyond the local. It means you recognize, albeit, in a small way, that industrial agriculture isn't always the best thing for human health or the health of the planet.

Your decision and desire to garden may not be an act of rebellion—it may simply be a fun hobby or a nod to getting healthier—but it is a small symbol of what may be wrong with a larger system that relies on petrochemicals and science more than it considers the health and well-being of its consumers and land.

It should be noted that industrial agriculture has had some advantages: the ability to feed more people more consistently and conveniently is undeniable. But it is also undeniably true that the industry has become politically entrenched, wielding enormous amounts of power in determining what and how we eat. As many people are aware, only five corporations control the vast majority of our food supply, leaving an increasingly vulnerable population at the mercy of corporate boardroom decisions. One small garden plot will not change the world, but it is a start, an acknowledgment of our desires to live in a kinder, gentler, and more sustainable world.

However, organic gardening is more than just abstract thinking; it is about getting one's hands dirty, literally, working with the earth and the weather to feed the body, mind, and soul. It's difficult to overestimate the amount of respect one gains for where our food comes from until they work on a farm or in a garden. If your children's only exposure to food is through shrink-wrapped packages or orderly supermarket shelves, they are unlikely to develop a strong respect for nature.

Gardening and farming demonstrate the ethics of hard work—they reveal the "fruits of our labor."," literally speaking—and raises strong moral concerns about waste and carelessness. It's easy to dismiss a shriveling head of lettuce in the fridge if you bought it for a few dollars at a corporate-run grocery store; it's nearly impossible to dismiss something you planted, nurtured, and harvested yourself.

Not only do gardeners begin to see waste as an opportunity—compost, anyone?—but we also begin to cringe at the sheer amount of plastic generated by a single trip to the grocery store. Your organic vegetables are never exposed to plastic or the inside of a refrigerator truck, resulting in a nearly zero carbon footprint.

On that note, I'd like to make a quick digression. Clearly, even if supplemented by trips to the farmers' market, it is unlikely that the grocery store can be avoided entirely when gardening on a small plot in the backyard. Still, within that realm, we can make choices that continue to reverberate in some of the same ways that our own decision to garden has.

Look for local producers; avoid out-of-season produce; and buy organic whenever possible. Even the largest grocery store chains, such as Wal-Mart, have begun to carry locally grown or made products and have expanded their still somewhat meager organic offerings. If you don't live in a community with a large farmers' market or easy access to local, fresh producers, don't worry: you can vote with your wallet by purchasing products that are good for you, your family, and the environment.

It is up to us to make small changes in our own lives that have a larger impact on the community and the world. As anthropologist Margaret Mead once said, "Never doubt that a small community of thoughtful, committed citizens can change the world; indeed, it is the only thing that has ever done so." Our purchasing power is derived not only from our wallets but also from our values. We can do our small part and encourage others to do the same.

Though some of the calls to go organic can be unreasonable—extreme localism is unsustainable as a means of feeding a growing population—there is still much to be gained by engaging in the struggle over plate politics, not to mention a nation (remember: our ancestors were hungry much of the time).

In the end, no single idea or action can change the history of industrial agriculture, but simply leaving it at that is dangerous, serving as a passive invitation to allow more genetically modified organisms, processed foods, and corporate control into our grocery stores and homes. It is to withdraw from the table's communion and to isolate ourselves from new and old neighbors.

Believing that food has meaning beyond the purely physical paves the way for the development of a healthier, more environmentally sound, and ultimately more humane food system.

After all, the food you grow in your backyard tastes really, really good! It is also undeniably beneficial to you and your community. Finally, it is some of the most rewarding and enjoyable hard work you will ever do. Breaking bread together represents the best of what humanity has to offer. Good appetite!

Conclusion

Organic vegetable gardening from your own backyard is one of the most rewarding and long-lasting endeavors you can undertake. Many of the numerous benefits to both body and soul that come from gardening include planning a garden, preparing the soil, nurturing plants, outwitting pests, harvesting, preserving, and preparing meals. You are not only improving your own, your friends, and your family's health and well-being, but you are also actively contributing to the creation of a healthier environment and a better world.

I hope you enjoyed this seasonal journey and now have the confidence and knowledge to start your own backyard garden. Advice on how to set up a garden; how to prepare the soil; how to plant (and when and what to plant); how to combat pests and diseases; how to harvest and preserve; and how to succession plant to ensure continuous garden growth are all available. Furthermore, the numerous benefits of starting an organic garden are discussed throughout, ranging from avoiding petrochemicals and their negative effects to fostering tastier and more nutritious food.

If you enjoyed this book and learned something from it, please take the time to rate it on Amazon. This will inspire others to start their own backyard projects, spreading health and happiness, just as your organic vegetable garden serves as a beacon in your larger community.

www.ingramcontent.com/pod-product-compliance
Lightning Source LLC
LaVergne TN
LVHW050654200726
843506LV00010B/1509